MORE PRAISE FOR
DR. ART'S GUIDE TO SCIENCE

"As a teacher, I appreciate how Dr. Art connects science standards with my students' daily lives. By showing how science ideas fit together, he makes science much easier to understand for both students and teachers."
Ms. Rhonda Spidell, Albert Einstein Distinguished Educator, National Science Foundation

"How can dancers at a 50th Anniversary Ball explain states of matter, and why do we live on the Goldilocks Planet? *Dr. Art's Guide To Science* explains these and many other basic and big ideas in science in ways that are simple, elegant, and fun."
Dr. Richard Vineyard, president, Council of State Science Supervisors

"Written in an engaging style with eye-catching graphics, Dr. Art's Guide is fun, informative and educational, all at the same time. I look forward to using this book in my work with both pre-service and practicing teachers!"
Dr. Jerome M. Shaw, assistant professor of science education, University of California Santa Cruz

"This book will immerse readers of all ages in the joy of science. They will develop a deep understanding of how the life, physical, and earth sciences explain our world."
Mr. Eric Packenham, director, Building a Presence for Science, National Science Teachers Association

"This is a timely resource for science teachers, parents, and those who teach science in an informal setting. It gives you the background, the connections, and the next steps. A must-have for your science resource library."
Dr. Jo Anne Vasquez, president, National Science Education Leadership Association

"*Dr. Art's Guide To Science* provides an engaging exploration of why science matters and how science works. Its great balance of big ideas and effective vignettes make key science concepts accessible to today's students."
Dr. Len Simutis, director, goENC.com (formerly Eisenhower National Clearinghouse for Mathematics and Science Education)

"This superb book helps us think about how our planet works, who we are, and what is life. Dr. Art invites us to jump in and Try Science."
Dr. Eric Marshall, director, TryScience.org

Dr. Art's Guide to Science

Connecting Atoms, Galaxies, and Everything in Between

Art Sussman, Ph.D.

JOSSEY-BASS
A Wiley Imprint
www.josseybass.com

In partnership with WestEd

Published by Jossey-Bass
A Wiley Imprint
989 Market Street, San Francisco, CA 94103-1741 www.josseybass.com

Design: Jack Macy

Illustrations: Emiko Paul/Echo Medical Media

Portions of this book have previously appeared in *Dr. Art's Guide to Planet Earth*, copyright
©2000 by WestEd. WestEd, a nonprofit research, development, and service agency, works with
education and other communities to promote excellence, achieve equity, and improve learning
for children, youth, and adults. For more information about WestEd: www.wested.org

Photo credits appear on p. viii.

Jossey-Bass books and products are available through most bookstores. To contact Jossey-Bass
directly call our Customer Care Department within the U.S. at 800-956-7739, outside the U.S. at
317-572-3986, or fax 317-572-4002. Jossey-Bass also publishes its books in a variety of electronic
formats. Some content that appears in print may not be available in electronic books.

Cataloging-in-publication data has been applied for.
ISBN 13: 978-0-7879-8326-0
ISBN 10: 0-7879-8326-8
Printed in the United States of America
FIRST EDITION
HB Printing   10 9 8 7 6 5 4 3 2 1

TABLE OF CONTENTS

Photographic and Artwork Credits

This page constitutes a continuation of the copyright page.
Key: **Source** page (subject) Photographer

Brand X Pictures
Cover (red rock and trees) Morey Milbradt
John D. Byrd, Mississippi State University
www.forestryimages.org 235 (kudzu)
California Academy of Sciences
161 (ants) Dong Lin © 2005 California Academy of Sciences; 195
Dr. Lloyd Glenn Ingles © California Academy of Sciences
Canadian Museum of Civilization (CMC)
3 (pyramid) © CMC photo Frank Corcoran, no. D2004-6191
CERN: European Organization for Nuclear Research
94 (compact linear collider) Laurent Guiraud/CERN
Corbis
160 (Martin Luther King, Jr.) Bettmann/CORBIS
Janet Delaney
ix
Dennis Kunkel Microscopy, Inc.
16 (penicillin); 17, 25 (anthrax); 91 (blood cell); 163, 240 (paramecium);
163 (flower cells); 164 (muscle, nerve & leaf cells); 190 (bee)
Digital Stock
3 (cliff dwellings); 28; 46 (thermal pool); 160 (rocks)
Digital Vision Ltd.
18 (cars); 78 (power plant); 121; 151; 223 (inset); 226 (garbage,
polluted water); 227 (ozone); 234 (fire); 235 (pipe, logging)
Jim Ekstrom
http://science.exeter.edu/jekstrom/default.html 91 (bee head)
Getty Images
Cover (stars) StockTrek; cover, 87, 90, 243 (spiral galaxy) StockTrek;
cover, 86 (astronaut) StockTrek; v, 1 (beakers) Greg Pease; i–iii, v, 27
(water) Digital Vision; vi, 105 (Earth) StockTrek; 1 (inset) Paul
Cooklin; 3 (teepee) Geostock; 3 (huts) Ingo Jezierski; 7 (test tubes)
Mel Yates; 12 (cells) Darlyne Murawski; 29 (water) Digital Vision;
35 (coal train) Don Farrall; 35 (oxygen) Thinkstock; 44 (bubbles)
Digital Vision; 51 Digital Vision; 57 (fire) Izzy Schwartz; 57 (cars)
Steve Allen; 57 (runner) Comstock Images; 60 Photodisc
Collection; 75, 242 (magnet) Harald Sund; 79 Digital Vision; 85
(moon surface) StockTrek; 90 (Earth) StockTrek; 90 (SF Bay) StockTrek;
94 (stars) StockTrek; 94 (bomb detonation) StockTrek; 94
(Hiroshima) Archive Holding Inc.; 97, 104 (stars) StockTrek; 98
StockTrek; 99 (dinosaur) Stephen Wilkes; 102 StockTrek; 106-07
(Earth) StockTrek; 132 (microwave) Stockdisc; 132 (green light)
Don Farrall; 134 (rainbow) Robert Glusic; 136 (highway) Jeremy
Woodhouse; 137 (greenhouse) Sami Sarkis; 139 (geyser)
image100; 139 (earthquake) Doug Menuez; 141 StockTrek; 153,
241 (mushrooms) Don Farrall; 154, 241 (cougar) Photodisc
Collection; 160 (stars) StockTrek; 161 (students) Flying Colours Ltd;
166 (lab) David Buffington; 167 (steak) Comstock Images; 167,
180 (beans) Photodisc Collection; 167 (sushi) Daisuke Morita; 172
(cells) Dr Stanley Flegler; 172 (embryo) Dr Fred Hossler; 176
(mother/daughter) Digital Vision; 183 (computers) Kevin Phillips;
186 Hulton Collection; 194 (insect) Annie Griffiths Belt; 196
(impalas) Natphotos; 196 (lions) MIMOTITO; 197 General
Photographic Agency; 199 David Young-Wolff; 200 (snail) Bob
Elsdale; 236 (aspirin) Burke/Triolo Productions; 239 Digital Vision
iStockphoto
Cover, vii, 159 (bacteria) Monika Wisniewska; cover (atom) Perttu
Sironen; cover (bee) Roel Dillen; vi, 63, 70, 84 (lightning) Linda
Bair; vii, 181 (fossil) Bob Ainsworth; vii, 205 (hoodoos) Steve Geer;
vii, 223 (road) Peter Chen; 7 (warning) Dan Brandenburg; 38

Alexander Briel Perez; 45 (tree) Paulus Rusyanto; 47 (definition)
Nurkemala Muliani; 61-62 (purple background) Benoit Beauregar
64 (apple) Jorge Sa; 66 (x-ray) Peter Nguyen; 70 (meter) Stan
Rohrer; 88 (baby) Kenneth C. Zirkel; 88 (theatre) John Bohannon
108 Mark Rossmore; 114, 245 Carol Gering; 132 (satellite dish)
BlaneyPhoto; 133 Andrzej Tokarski; 136 (windmills) Jason Stitt;
143-144 (background) Anneclaire Le Royer; 143-144 (blue inset)
Peter Hansen; 158 (lichen background) Paul Cowan; 174 (neon
DNA) Valerie Loiseleux; 180 (background) Charissa Wilson; 183
(traffic) Mika Makkonen; 183 (store) Sean Locke; 185 (rock) Dani
Norman; 185 (forest) Jordan Ayan; 190 (snake) Brad Thompson;
194 (peaches) Michel de Nijs; 204 (background) Stasys Eidiejus;
212 Andrew Krasnov; 222 (background) Martin Hendriks; 227,
235 (soil) Ben Thomas; 234 (park) Pierre Janssen; 236 (panda)
Paiwei Wei; 237 (dragonfly) Andrei Mihalcea
Louisiana Superdome
40
D.L. Mark
32, 35 (dome)
NASA
vi, 23, 83, 85, 95, 203, 219 (stars) NASA, ESA and A. Nota
(STScI); 4 J. Spencer (Lowell Observatory) and NASA; 18, 26 (sur
NASA Jet Propulsion Laboratory (NASA-JPL); 48 (space shuttle)
NASA; 61-62 (sun) NASA-JPL; 66 (Tarantula nebula) The Hubble
Heritage Team (AURA / STScI / NASA); 82 (Saturn) NASA and Th
Hubble Heritage Team (STScI/AURA); 87 (Milky Way-top) NASA;
90 (universe) NASA, ESA, R. Windhorst (Arizona State University
and H. Yan (Spitzer Science Center, Caltech); 90 (whirlpool galax
NASA and The Hubble Heritage Team (STScI/AURA); 106 (Mars
Rover) NASA-JPL; 215, 222, 240 (asteroid) NASA-JPL; 217, 243
(impact) Don Davis/NASA
National Institute of Standards and Technology
32, 91 (cobalt atoms)
National Oceanic and Atmospheric Administration
231 (ice core) Lonnie Thompson, Byrd Polar Research Center, Th
Ohio State University. Also NOAA Paleoclimatology Program /
Department of Commerce
National Park Service
160 (cave) Peter Jones
Natural History Museum, London
213 (mosasaurus); 213 (pteranodon); 214; 217 (tektites)
PhotoDisc
v, 13, 90-91 (flower); vi, 127 (greenhouses); vi, 145 (spider); vii, 12
(sunflowers); 29 (clouds); 45, 63 (sand inset); 46 (hurricane); 46 (tiger
48, 242 (lava); 50 (oil rig); 78 (power lines); 78 (mushroom cloud);
78 (sun); 109; 112; 116; 119 (turtle); 120; 124; 126 (lava inset); 12
(cloud inset); 140; 146 (cactus, sea anemones, flamingoes); 148;
150 (cheetah); 158 (anemone inset); 160 (butterfly); 161 (trees); 18
(lava flow); 194, 204 (peacock); 196 (sea stars, seals); 227 (cheeta
Photo Resources Hawaii
236 (bird) Jack Jeffrey
Wim van Egmond
15 (cactus leaf); 18 (flea)
Virtual Fossil Museum
www.fossilmuseum.net 185, 243 (fossil); 187; 213 (ammonite)
Wonderfile
81 © stockbyte; 160 (Socrates) © Image Source

viii

About the Author

Dr. Art Sussman received his Ph.D. in Biochemistry from Princeton University. He continued to perform scientific research at Oxford University, Harvard Medical School, and the University of California. For the past 30 years, he has helped students, teachers, and the general public understand science as it affects them in their daily lives. Dr. Art works at WestEd (one of ten regional educational laboratories created by Congress) to improve science education at local, state, and national levels. He helps states with their science education standards, and shows how you can teach and learn required science content in ways that are understandable, interesting, and fun.

DVD

Dr. Art Does Science is a 90-minute DVD that models enjoyable and effective ways to teach important science concepts. It features the complete "Dr. Art's Planet Earth Show," a theatre-style presentation that combines exciting science demonstrations with audience participation to teach how our planet works.

Dr. Art Does Science also features 11 chapters in which experiments, demonstrations, and animations illuminate key topics such as electromagnetism, chemical reactions, the greenhouse effect, and respiration. Ordering details and more information are available on the guidetoscience website (see below).

Website

Go to www.guidetoscience.net to enhance your *Dr. Art's Guide to Science* experience. This website includes experiments, animations, lesson plans, and more intriguing science ideas for each of the book's chapters. Learn the meaning of key science words, and hear them pronounced by a computer programmed to sound just like Dr. Art. Also confirm the location of this book's Just Kidding things, such as the computer in the previous sentence.

Acknowledgements

Many people helped me write this book, but two people made it beautiful. Emiko Paul, the book's illustrator, turned my sketchy descriptions into elegant illustrations and delightful cartoon images that convey the essence of the science ideas. Jack Macy, the book's graphic designer, brilliantly combined the text, illustrations, and photographs so that page after page stands out as a work of art. They both greatly increased my enjoyment of the book as we created it together.

Dr. Art's Guide to Science would not exist without the essential help of Michelle Kirk and Cheeta Llanes. Michelle researched, found, and obtained essentially all the book's photographs. This task involved knowing the science, having an eye for beauty, tracking down sources, filling out the legal purchase forms, and organizing the more than 225 photos. Cheeta Llanes provided personal and professional support, including researching science content, editing, and helping me focus on the essential science ideas.

Many science colleagues helped keep the science writing both accurate and understandable. I have to admit that I occasionally ignored their advice, so I take full responsibility for any errors.

Kathy DiRanna helped me launch the first chapters. She then continued to help me recognize the places where students and teachers get confused, and figure out how we could guide readers to clearer understandings. My favorite physicist, Helen Quinn, reviewed the physical science chapters, and saved me from writing things that would drive a physicist crazy.

This publication was supported in part by the United States Department of Education (Award Number R319A000006). I gratefully acknowledge that assistance. Any opinions, interpretations, or conclusions expressed in this book are those of the author, and do not necessarily reflect those of the U. S. Department of Education, or of WestEd.

I also thank Glenn Herrick and Judy Scotchmoor for their help with the evolution chapters, and Michael Daehler for his physics review. Libby Rognier also reviewed the manuscript, and did research for the website. Lynn Murphy gave valuable publishing assistance. Finally, I gratefully acknowledge the outstanding support of my favorite employer, WestEd, and the help of the Jossey-Bass team, especially Christie Hakim who championed the book, and coordinated its publication.

WHY SCIENCE?

?
?
Why?

First Scientists

At one time in your life, you probably drove everyone around you crazy because you kept asking "Why." Why is water wet? Why does it become a solid at cold temperatures? Why does sugar disappear when I put it in water? Why can't I eat as much sugar as I can possibly stuff in my mouth? And, of course, why is the sky blue?

If you observe a kitten or a puppy, you will see the same curiosity. Young animals will poke their noses into everything to learn more about their world. A kitten may become so curious about its tail that it will spin in circles trying to catch it. Curiosity can be a lot like playing.

Curiosity has helped humans become very successful as a species. Because we can learn about our world and teach each other what we have learned, we have been able to spread to all parts of our planet. We have figured out ways to live in deserts, rainforests, mountaintops, and snow. We have figured out how to hunt fierce animals, stay warm, and grow our own food.

BIG IDEA

Curiosity helped humans succeed as a species.

Our earliest ancestors included scientists. These early scientists did not wear white laboratory coats. Still, we can call them scientists because they carefully observed their environments, and they experimented with the best ways to get food, build shelters, and heal each other. Like scientists today, our ancestors communicated what they learned, and used their group knowledge to explain the past. They could even begin to predict the future.

About 2,000 years ago, the Maya in Central America used detailed observations of the Sun, Moon, and Venus to develop a very accurate calendar. They could predict eclipses of the Sun and Moon, as well as easily know the beginnings of the four

different seasons. Without metal tools or wheels, they built huge, marvelous structures that still stand today.

One of the most famous Mayan structures is a pyramid called El Castillo where the Maya combined their calendar knowledge with their building skills. One special feature of this building is that at the start of spring and autumn, the sunlight catches the top of the edge of the western stairway. The sunlight then descends the edge of the staircase and reaches a carved serpent's head at the bottom. This special effect makes it appear as if a long serpent is creeping down the stairway (the photo above shows people still coming today to stare at the "light snake" descending the stairs on the left side of the pyramid).

Like the Maya, people all over the planet were using science skills to succeed in their different environments. However, modern science did not begin until about 500 years ago in Europe. In that time and place, people began using more tools, mathematics, logic, and communication than they ever had before to ask and answer questions about the world.

Like other humans, European scientists were trying to understand the Sun, Moon, stars, and planets. In the year 1609, the telescope had just

We have figured out ways to live in deserts, rainforests, mountaintops, and snow.

been invented in Holland. Galileo, in Italy, read about it on the Internet, and that same year made a telescope that was seven times stronger.[1] In 1610, carefully examining the night sky with his new tool, he became the first person to see small dots traveling around Jupiter.

By carefully observing these dots and how they traveled, he proved that they were four different moons of Jupiter, and that each one had its own path around that distant planet.

This was the first time that humans knew that our Moon is not the only moon, and that Earth is not the center around which everything moves. At that time, almost everyone believed that the Sun and the planets all traveled around the Earth. Earth was not just a planet. It was the center of everything. It was the only thing that had a moon. Now we knew that at least one other planet has moons, and that those moons travel around Jupiter, not around Earth.

Soon, people all over Europe were using telescopes, and trying to understand everything that they could see. Watching these four moons travel around Jupiter helped humans realize that Earth travels around the Sun. We realized that Earth and the other planets travel around the Sun. This new understanding was a huge change from the old belief that the Sun and all the planets travel around Earth.

The telescope taught us a huge science lesson about our place in the universe. Even more important, science developed from this way of combining observations, tools, logic, mathematics, and communication. As science grew, it became more than a way to satisfy our curiosity. Science could save lives.

BIG IDEA

The telescope changed the way we see ourselves.

Curiosity Saved The Human

Without science, I would not be alive today, which means you would not be reading this book. When I was three years old, I had a dangerous ear infection, and I was rushed

[1] Just kidding. The first telephone, electric lines, and computers would not be invented until hundreds of years later. The STOP & THINK section at the end of this chapter explains why this science book has "just kidding" things in it.

by ambulance to the hospital. I had a very high fever, and the infection was moving toward my brain. Fortunately, about 20 years before I was born, a scientist named Alexander Fleming had discovered natural antibiotics. Just a couple of years before I came into the world, scientists figured out how to make enough of these drugs to treat sick people. Penicillin, the first antibiotic discovered by scientists, saved my life.

Science and technology have continued to change practically everything about our lives. The food we eat, how we cook it, how we prevent and cure diseases, and how we entertain ourselves have all changed in amazing ways since the 1950s when I was a mischievous teenager.

Think about how we communicate with each other. My 1950s apartment had only one telephone. If I wanted to use it, I had to stand right next to its location on the kitchen wall. And sometimes I could not use it because we had a party line.

Party lines were not fun. Since there were not enough phone lines to serve everybody, we had to share our phone line with two other households that we did not even know. If I picked up the phone and heard a voice, I had to wait for someone from one of those other homes to hang up before I could use the phone.

We never dreamed that one day we could have phones to take with us wherever we went. Probably nobody in the 1950s imagined that future phones could be mobile, take photographs, and send those

Tilly Smith, a ten year-old British schoolgirl, was playing with her family on Maikhao Beach in Thailand on December 26, 2004. She noticed that the water "started to go funny." Remembering a science lesson she had learned in school just 2 weeks earlier, she screamed at her family to get off the beach because a tsunami could be coming.

The Smiths ran off the beach, and warned other people. They raced to their hotel, and went up to the third floor. There they watched in horror as three tsunami waves crashed into the hotel. The beach and hotel swimming pool filled with surging water, palm trees, beds, and other debris.

British newspapers reported that Tilly's science knowledge and quick actions had saved herself, her family, and 100 other people.

photos with text messages to people all over the world. That was too far out a fantasy for any of us to imagine.

Why Should We Learn Science?

While science makes it possible to have antibiotics, cell phones, and computers, you don't need to understand science to be able to use these modern miracles. Yet, our society has decided that everybody who goes to school needs to learn science. Nations all around the world test their students in science, and compare the scores to keep track of how well their students know science. In the United States, political and business leaders are very concerned because tests show that American students perform poorly in science compared with students from many other countries.

Still, that does not answer the question—why do we need to learn science? Business leaders know that many jobs require a solid science background. They complain that they have a hard time finding workers who have strong enough science skills and knowledge. From your point of view, this means that knowing science can help you get some very interesting, satisfying, enjoyable, and well-paying jobs.

Knowing science will help you make the best decisions for your community, your country, and the planet.

I have one of those kinds of jobs. I work as a science educator, which means that I have training and experience in both science and teaching. As a science educator, I help teachers learn the science they need to know, and I help them learn the best ways to teach science knowledge and skills. I also help states decide what science topics and skills to teach at different grade levels.

Science educators agree that studying science can help students get much better jobs. But we think there is an even more important reason why everyone needs to understand science. It is so science educators like us can have jobs and sell books about learning science.

Okay, that is not our main reason. Science educators think that people need to understand science so they can make the best decisions for themselves, for their family and local community, for their country, and for the one planet that is our home. We call this "science literacy for citizens."

Science can help you make the best decisions for yourself. What kind of food should you eat? How can you stay healthy, and what should you do if you have different kinds of illness? How do smoking cigarettes or taking other drugs affect your body? If you hear about something from a friend or television or the Internet, how can you check if it is true or not? Should you use astrology to decide if someone would be a good friend, or even a possible romantic interest?

SURGEON GENERAL'S WARNING: Smoking Causes Lung Cancer, Heart Disease, Emphysema, And May Complicate Pregnancy.

Knowing science will help you make the best decisions for yourself.

Science can help you answer those questions about your personal decisions. We also think that science can help you make the best decisions for your local community, your country, and for the planet. Should you care about how much energy and water you use? Should your community provide public transportation, and what would be the best ways? What should be done with all the waste products that your family/town/city produces? Are humans changing Earth's climate? If yes, should you do something about it, and what should you do?

I hope you agree that learning science is good for you, for your country, and for the world. As science educators, we think that learning science is important, and that it is fun. In a way, scientists are like children who never lose their curiosity, who keep on asking why. In science, you can sometimes have as much fun as a kitten catching her tail after running around in a circle.

Learning Science

I don't know what experiences you have had in learning science. I hope that you have explored science topics with your hands and with your mind. Science involves carefully observing the world and testing ideas to figure out how things work.

While I am a great believer in learning science by doing experiments, this book has very few experiments in it. Instead, the companion website (www.guidetoscience.net) includes experiments, animations, and other features that can take you deeper into the science. This book, *Dr. Art's Guide to Science*, provides the science background that you need, explaining the biggest ideas in science and how these ideas all fit together. These big ideas will help you understand what science is all about. As you read this book, things that you studied in school or saw on television will probably make sense to you in new and surprising ways. You may even discover that reading this book will change how you think about yourself and the world.

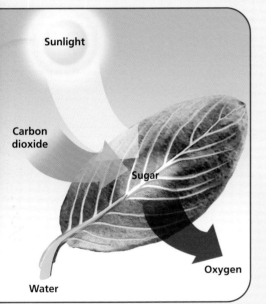

Sunlight

Carbon dioxide

Sugar

Oxygen

Water

As an example of what I mean, let's consider a big science idea called **photosynthesis**. Photosynthesis is what plants do to be able to live. Unlike animals, plants do not eat. Instead of eating, they use the energy from sunlight to make sugar. Plants then use this sugar to make all the chemicals and get all the energy they need.

By doing photosynthesis, plants take carbon dioxide gas from the air and combine it with water to make sugar. As shown in the illustration, they do this by capturing the energy from sunlight. Another very important part of photosynthesis is that plants give off oxygen as a result of this process.

Since science depends so much on accurate communication, scientists pay a lot of attention to the words they use. For example, in describing how plants get their energy, they did not want to always have to say "you know, the thing that plants do when they use the energy from sunlight to make sugar from carbon dioxide and water." So, they call it photosynthesis. Even though it is a 5-syllable word, it is still a lot shorter. Plus the name fits the process that it is describing. "Photo" means light, and "synthesize" means to make (you may have heard the word "synthetic," which means something that is made out of materials that humans have made).

Photosynthesis is so important that textbooks and school systems want to make sure that students know the word. They usually do that by asking a test question that looks like this:

> *The process by which plants use energy from the Sun to make sugar is called*
> *   a) perspiration*
> *   b) respiration*
> *   c) photosynthesis*
> *   d) aggravation*
> *   e) photolysis*

I agree that you should know and recognize the word photosynthesis. However, if you just learn it as a vocabulary word that you have to memorize, you are not going to understand it because all you have done is memorize a word and some phrases that are associated with that word (make sugar, energy from sunlight). Then, you will forget the word because it is too hard to remember a word that you do not really understand, especially when you keep getting new words to memorize.

In contrast, science is about understanding. Memorizing some words is necessary, but understanding is the most important part.

What would it mean to really understand photosynthesis? First of all, it is not just a word in science textbooks. Photosynthesis happens all around you. Look at the sunlight shining on a green plant, tree, bush, or blade of grass. Every one of these plants is doing photosynthesis as you are watching it.

1 Photosynthesis happens all around us.

Second, through photosynthesis, plants take light energy from the Sun and package it as chemical energy in sugar. No animal can perform this remarkable feat. All of us animals depend on plants to capture the Sun's energy and store it in a form that we can use. From the point of view of Earth's organisms, photosynthesis is the most important thing that any organism does. Plants need photosynthesis to live, and so do we.

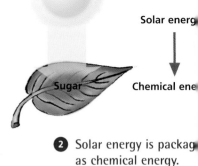

Solar energy

Sugar   Chemical ene

2 Solar energy is packag as chemical energy.

Third, plants give off oxygen as a result of photosynthesis. Earth's original atmosphere did not have oxygen gas. Today, oxygen makes up 21% of our atmosphere. All that oxygen got into the atmosphere as a result of photosynthesis. Not only does this 5-syllable word explain where animals get their food, it also explains how we get the air that we breathe.

Try to remember to stop the next time you pass some grass, bushes, or trees in the sunlight. Even though you cannot see it, that green living being is putting oxygen into the air around you. You breathe in that oxygen and breathe out carbon dioxide. The plant takes in the carbon dioxide to make the food that supports the communities of living organisms. You are very tightly connected with plant life. Plants and animals are partners in Earth's web of life.

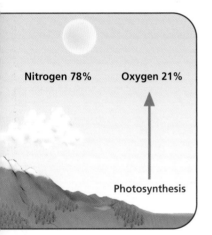

Nitrogen 78%   Oxygen 21%

Photosynthesis

3 Photosynthesis makes the oxygen we breathe.

Most of us live in cities and suburbs where we mainly see the human-made world rather than the world of nature. Eating food from supermarkets and restaurants and spending our time in buildings and vehicles,

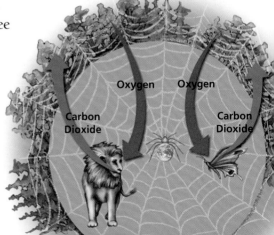

Oxygen   Oxygen

Carbon
Dioxide

Carbon
Dioxide

we may never know a very important part of who we are. By studying photosynthesis, we learn a huge lesson about ourselves. Like all animals, we depend on plants and the Sun's energy. We are all part of Earth's web of life.

The Science Coming Of Age Story

In most cultures, young people have "coming of age" experiences. Their parents and the wise leaders of their community make sure they know the history, customs, and rules of their group. You may have experienced this through your religion or through a community social group.

We live in a science-based society. Practically everything that we touch and do has been shaped in some way by science. However, I bet that you did not have a science "coming of age" experience. Nobody said to you, "We think it is time to make sure that you know what science says about where we came from, who we are, and where we are going."

Well, it turns out that science has an amazing and inspiring description of where we came from, who we are, and where we are going. That is what I hope you will find in this book.

All we are saying is : Give Science A Chance

Some of you know that you are already interested in science. That is great. I hope this book takes that interest further and into surprising directions. Some of you may think you are not interested in science. Perhaps you had bad or no experiences with science. Try to read this book with an open mind. As John Lennon, one of the famous rock and roll Beatles, wrote in a song, "Give Science a Chance."

STOP & THINK

You probably have much more experience reading fiction books than a nonfiction book like this. Of course, the actual process of reading the words is the same. Don't get fooled by that. It takes some different reading skills to get the most enjoyment and learning from a nonfiction book.

With a good fiction book, sometimes you want to read faster and faster. What is going to happen next? Will the heroine escape? You forget about yourself, and escape into a fantasy world that the author has created.

With this book, I don't want you to forget about yourself. I want you to be aware of what you are thinking and what you know. As you read, I hope you are figuring out if the ideas make sense to you or not. Are they totally new ideas? Do they fit with what you know? Do they make you think about something in a new way?

You might find yourself reading slower and slower, rather than faster and faster. You might read about a new idea, and then go back a page or more to see how this new idea connects with something you read before. This book will not help you escape into a fantasy world. Instead, I want to take you deeper into reality, and show you how to look at the world with different eyes.

You may remember that I pretended that in 1609 Galileo found out about the telescope by reading about it on the Internet. No way! He lived about 350 years before the first home computer. Why did I do that?

One reason is that I have a weird sense of humor. I admit that. Another reason is that I want to remind you to think about what you are reading. Watch out for my tricks. I will never lie to you about something important, but I will put in "just kidding" stuff like Galileo using the Internet. In case you are not sure, the guidetoscience website has a "just kidding" section where I will admit to all my mischief, such as the title of John Lennon's song.

By the way, "Think about what you are reading" is good advice for other things that you read. Especially if they do not have a "just kidding" section.

www.guidetoscience.net

TWO PLUS TWO EQUALS HIP-HOP

Bee + Flower = Honey

Chapter 2 – *Two Plus Two Equals Hip-Hop*

Science Ideas Come In Different Sizes

In the last chapter we talked about photosynthesis. That is a really big science idea. It helps us understand how plants can live without eating anything. Since animals cannot make their own food, they depend on eating plants or eating other animals that eat plants. Thus, photosynthesis is a very big idea that helps us understand how life works on planet Earth.

One thing you should know about scientists is that they pay a lot of attention to details. A big idea such as photosynthesis does not just pop into somebody's head. Many scientists spent huge amounts of time observing and experimenting with all kinds of plants and trees. Over time, all the things they learned helped them understand that plants use sunlight to combine carbon dioxide and water to make sugar.

The mass of the tree does not come from the soil.

People used to think that plants eat soil just like animals eat plants. Around the time that Galileo was looking at Jupiter's moons, Jan Baptista van Helmont did an experiment to figure out where the mass of a tree comes from. He planted a young, willow tree weighing five pounds in a large pot containing 200 pounds of soil. He carefully watered the tree, and did not let anything else enter the soil. After five years, the tree had grown so much that it now weighed 169 pounds. However, the soil weighed only two ounces less than it had weighed at the start of the experiment.

169 POUNDS

5 POUNDS

200 POUNDS

200 POUNDS

5 Years Later   Start

Where did the 164 pounds that the tree gained come from? With this experiment, Helmont proved that the mass of the tree did not come from the soil. He concluded that the 164 pounds of plant (wood, leaves, bark, and roots) came from the water. Actually, his conclusion was wrong. Remember that photosynthesis tells us that plants use both carbon dioxide and water to make the sugar that they then use to make everything else. It turns out that most of the mass of a tree (or any plant) comes from the carbon dioxide, not from the water.

Plants get this carbon dioxide from the air through tiny openings in their leaves. The fact that plants have structures to take in carbon dioxide and give off oxygen is part of the evidence for photosynthesis. These openings are important for plants. However, compared to the huge idea of photosynthesis, the idea that leaves have openings is not such a big idea.

Note the nine openings shown in this electron microscope photo of a cactus leaf.

As you can see, science has lots of ideas and information. Some of them are really big ideas that are very important, while others are not so big or important. The following sentences include some ideas we

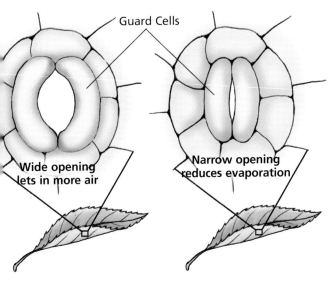

w Carbon Dioxide

Hot Dry Day

Guard Cells

Wide opening lets in more air

Narrow opening reduces evaporation

If the air has less than the usual amount of carbon dioxide, the plant's air openings may get bigger to let in more air. On hot dry days, the air openings may become smaller to prevent too much water from evaporating out of the plant. The leaves have special cells called "guard cells" that can make the openings bigger or smaller.

have discussed. I have listed them in order starting with the biggest ideas down to the smallest ones I have mentioned:

Practically all living things on Earth depend on plants capturing energy from the Sun to make sugar by combining carbon dioxide and water.

Earth's original atmosphere had essentially no free oxygen. Today's atmosphere has oxygen because of photosynthesis.

Plants have openings in their leaves for gases to enter and leave.

The openings in the leaves can get larger or smaller.

The plant cells that make the openings smaller or larger are called guard cells.

The biggest ideas are obviously important. We care about having food to eat and oxygen to breathe. The smaller ideas and facts are important in a different way. Scientists generally figure out the big ideas by discovering or learning lots of smaller ideas, and seeing how they fit together. Scientists also need to know a lot of details if they want to use their knowledge to change things, such as cure a disease.

The science of diseases provides another example of science ideas that have different sizes. Doctors and scientists studied diseases for hundreds of years without realizing that small, invisible organisms were causing most of those diseases. In the late 1800's, the French scientist Louis Pasteur and the German scientist Robert Koch

This green mold makes penicillin, an antibiotic that saves human lives.

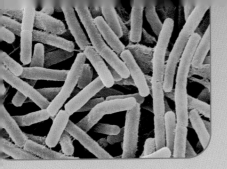

This is an electron microscope photo of the bacteria that cause anthrax.

investigated two diseases, anthrax and tuberculosis. They proved that a specific bacterium[1] causes anthrax, and that a different bacterium causes tuberculosis (often called TB). Soon, they and other scientists found that many other diseases are caused by bacteria. They also discovered that some diseases are caused by even smaller germs called viruses.

By investigating the details of many diseases, scientists proved that many diseases are caused by very small organisms that can be seen only with powerful microscopes. This important, big idea became known as the germ theory of disease. Scientists developed this theory by getting lots of detailed information about many different diseases. For each disease, they learned details about which germ causes that disease, how that germ makes us sick, and how it travels from one person to the next. For example, they learned that yellow fever is caused by a virus, and that a specific kind of mosquito carries the virus from one person to another. This understanding of yellow fever is a small idea compared with the much bigger idea that germs cause disease.

small IDEA

The *Aedes aegypti* mosquito transmits yellow fever.

The germ theory of disease tells us what kinds of things to look for as the causes of a disease. The smaller ideas and details help us figure out how we can use the science information in our daily lives. In the case of yellow fever, we learned that we can prevent that disease by getting rid of the mosquito that infects people with the yellow fever virus.

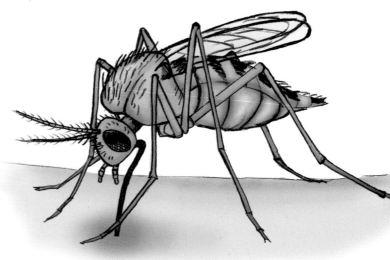

[1] *Bacterium* is the singular; *Bacteria* is the plural form of the word.

Thus, we need both the really big science ideas (such as photosynthesis and the germ theory of disease) and the smallest science facts. We need both sizes for doing science and for learning science. To teach and learn science well, we need to have a good balance of science ideas of many sizes. If there are too many small ideas and facts, we won't understand how they fit together, and we won't be able to remember them. On the other hand, if there are too few smaller ideas and facts, we really won't understand the big ideas. The examples and details help us understand where the big ideas came from and how they fit in the world.

My job as a science educator and book writer is to pick the most important big science ideas and combine them with just the right amount of smaller ideas. I hope you like my recipe. It continues now with an idea so huge that I call it an Awesome Idea.

An Awesome Idea

When I try to explain anything, I usually start talking about systems. We could be talking about a tree, planet Earth, transportation in a country, diseases, a forest, an ant, water, or the Sun. I like the word "systems" so much that I am surprised that I wrote the whole first chapter without using it.

A country has a transportation system with many parts.

The Sun is a system with many parts.

A flea is a system with many parts.

What do I mean by "systems," and why do I love to use the word? A **system** exists whenever two or more things combine or influence each other. We use the word "parts" for the things that combine or influence each other. We use the word "whole" to describe the new thing that exists because the parts have combined or connected with each other. A system occurs whenever parts combine or connect with each other to form a whole.

Does this sound like an awesome idea to you? Perhaps you are scratching your head or shaking it to signify no. I better explain what I mean.

Let's consider water as an example of a very simple system. Water is "H two O," which means that it consists of two parts of hydrogen (H) and one part of oxygen (O). If we run an electric current through water, we can break it down into the two gases hydrogen and oxygen. When we break down water, we get twice as much volume of hydrogen compared with the volume of oxygen. If we combine the hydrogen and oxygen back together, we get liquid water.

> A system exists whenever two or more things combine or influence each other.

Compare the parts to the whole. Hydrogen is a highly explosive gas. Oxygen is a gas that is needed for fires. When hydrogen and oxygen come together, they form water, a liquid that puts out fires. From a systems point of view, water is a whole that has properties that are very different from those of its parts.

Oxygen

Hydrogen

Water

BATTERY

Electricity splits water into hydrogen and oxygen gas.

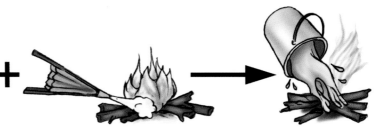

Hydrogen + Oxygen → Water

Water as a whole has properties that are very different than those of its parts.

Table salt provides another example. It is made of sodium and chlorine. Sodium is a shiny metal that bursts into flames when it touches water. Chlorine is a green poisonous gas. Put them together and you get a white solid that we love to put on our food. Salt is a whole that has **properties**[2] that are very different from those of its parts.

So now we know that systems, such as water and salt, are made of parts. We also know that systems can be very different from their parts.

Thinking in terms of systems is very useful because we are surrounded by all sorts of systems. In fact, each of us is our own little system. Each of us is made up of more than 200 kinds of cells. These nerve, skin, muscle, bone, and blood cells all join together to form an incredible system—an individual human person. All the structures that these cells form—our skin, muscles, bones, blood vessels, internal organs—work together as an interconnected whole system.

One important feature of systems is that each of the parts of a system is itself a system that is made of parts. How does that work? Okay, remember that you are a system. One of the parts of the "you system" is the circulatory system, which is the way blood moves throughout your body. This circulatory system is part of the bigger "you system," but it itself is a system with many parts.

---

[2] In science, the word *property* does not mean "something that a person owns." Look up *property* on page 245 if you are not sure of its scientific meaning.

The parts of the circulatory system include heart, veins, arteries, and blood cells. The heart, a part of the circulatory system, is also a system made of parts. Its parts include four different sections plus valves that open and close to make sure the blood flows into the correct section at the correct time. Each section of the heart is also a system that is made up of different kinds of cells such as muscle cell and nerve cells.

We could get dizzy visualizing all these systems within systems within systems that are inside each one of us. And the story does not end with us. We are not the biggest system around. Each of us is, in turn, part of many larger systems. Each of us is part of a family system. Each of us is part of an ecosystem. Each of us is part of an entire human system that is part of a system of life on this planet.

Why should we care about all these systems within systems within systems? It means that whenever we want to understand something,

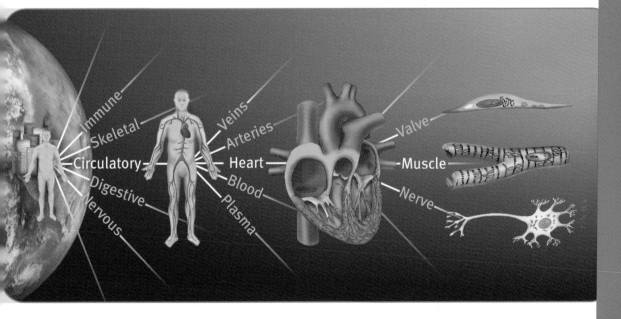

we can always investigate it as a system. We can learn a lot about it by figuring out what its parts are, and how these parts connect with each other. We can also learn a lot by figuring out how the system is itself a part of larger systems.

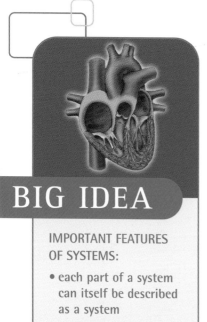

BIG IDEA

IMPORTANT FEATURES
OF SYSTEMS:

- each part of a system can itself be described as a system
- a system can be very different from its parts

Throughout this book, we will use this kind of "systems thinking" to understand many very different things. Systems thinking will help us understand what everything is made of, how our bodies work, and the ways that humans are affecting planet Earth.

Why Hip-Hop?

I called this chapter "Two Plus Two Equals Hip-Hop." What did I mean by that? Does that phrase have anything to do with systems?

Actually, it does. Remember that water has very different properties than oxygen and hydrogen. The parts of water are both gases, and they both support fires. In contrast, water is a liquid at normal temperatures and pressures, and it puts out fires. Salt also showed us that a whole system has properties that are very different than the parts.

Each of us is a system made out of arteries, red blood cells, stomach, and toenails. Your stomach is a part of who you are, but you are much more than your stomach. As a functioning interconnected whole, you have characteristics that do not exist in any of your parts. You have properties that go far beyond the qualities of your parts.

The popular saying "the whole is more than the sum of its parts" describes this important system feature. This popular saying is much deeper than it might first appear. When we say that the whole is more than the sum of its parts, we mean that the whole system has qualities that are different than those of the parts.

Think about it this way. We have all learned that two plus two equals four. When you hear that the whole is more than the sum of its parts, you might think that it means two plus two equals six. However, the difference between liquid water and hydrogen gas is not like the difference between six and four. It is not a difference in quantity. It is a difference in quality. It is not a difference in how much. It is a difference in what kind of thing it is.

Liquid water is as different from hydrogen gas as hip-hop is from a chair. Salt is as different from sodium metal as hip-hop is from homework. You are as different from your stomach as hip-hop is from an orange.

We express this reality by saying that the whole is qualitatively different from its parts. These qualitative differences are much more important than a mere increase in quantity. Now we can write our Awesome Systems Idea as:

The whole is **qualitatively** more than the sum of its parts.

Awesome Idea

SYSTEMS
Systems are made of parts that are themselves systems made of parts. Systems have properties that are qualitatively different than those of the parts.

Systems Can Make A Planet

Without knowing it, as a child you played with making systems. You probably played with toys that had a few parts from which you could make lots of very different things. With just a few different kinds of parts, you made all sorts of different things. These things were different from the simple building parts, and from each other.

In the next chapter, I will show you how we can make a whole planet such as Earth out of just three different kinds of parts. As you know, Earth has millions of different kinds of things. However, because parts can combine to form systems that have very different qualities, we can use just three parts to make all these different Earth things, including you and me. And that is why I say that systems is a truly awesome science idea.

STOP & THINK

Part of learning about our world through science involves learning new words. For example, photosynthesis is a word that scientists invented. You encounter it as part of learning science. The word photosynthesis does not have any other meaning besides its science meaning. You won't hear anybody say, "I have a photosynthesis that people who have red hair get angry more often than people with black hair."

In contrast, some words used in science are commonly used outside of science. Often their science meaning can be very different from their common meaning. In this chapter, I mentioned the germ theory of disease. The word "theory" was not invented by scientists. It is a common word. You could hear somebody say, "I have a theory that people who have red hair get angry more often than people with black hair."

That way of using the word "theory" is very different than how scientists use the word. In common language, a theory could be any idea about how one thing influences another thing. It could be a completely wacko idea (I have a theory that invisible Moon creatures cause thunder) to something very reasonable (I have a theory that people who grew up in large families tend to have more than two children).

Scientists use the word very differently. A scientific theory connects many facts and observations. It shows how they all make sense in terms of a very big idea. The germ theory of disease is not a wacko idea about Moon creatures. Instead, it explains thousands of observations of diseases such as the common cold, the flu, TB, measles, malaria, tetanus, and dental cavities.

In our common language, you would say that a fact is stronger than a theory. In science, the opposite is true. Since a science theory is supported by many facts, it actually is much more solid than any particular fact.

STOP & THINK
CONTINUED

As you read this book, notice when you encounter a new word. Try to figure out what it means by the way the word is used in the sentence. Also check to see if the nearby sentences or drawings help you figure out the meaning of the word.

You can also check to see if the word is in the "Glindex" at the back of this book (see page 240). I made up the word Glindex from the words Glossary (a place in a book that defines words that are used in that book) and Index (a place in a book that tells you where you can find specific words or ideas in that book). The Guide to Science Glindex tells you where you can find specific ideas and words, and helps you understand what they mean.

By the way, the guidetoscience website also has a Glindex that includes hearing a computer that was programmed to sound just like Dr. Art pronouncing the words.

Examples From The Glindex

System – a system exists whenever parts combine or connect with each other to form a whole. This whole is qualitatively more than the sum of its parts. You, your circulatory system, water, and table salt are all examples of systems. Pages 18-24.

Theory– a scientific explanation of the natural world that is based upon many different pieces and kinds of evidence. The germ theory of disease is an example. Pages 18, 25.

www.guidetoscience.net

WHAT'S THE MATTER?

Chapter 3 –
What's The Matter?

Millions From 92

On Earth, we can see and touch millions of different kinds of objects. Take a couple of minutes to list every kind of thing that you can think of. You could begin with everything that you can see, feel, touch, hear, and smell at this very moment. If you still have room on your paper, include in your list all the parts of those objects, and what you think those parts are made of. You could make the list bigger by including everything that you have experienced in just the last 24 hours, or by comparing your list with somebody else's list.

Look at all the different kinds of things on your list. What are they made of? In our history, humans have tried to understand how these millions of different kinds of things could exist. One explanation is that they could all be made from a much smaller number of basic building materials.

If you look at a city, you will see a very large number of buildings. You will notice that there are many different kinds of buildings, with a wide variety of shapes, sizes, and colors. However, all these different buildings are made using a much smaller number of construction materials—wood, glass, metal, concrete, paint, and plastic. Maybe the millions of different Earth things are all made from a much smaller number of construction materials.

BIG IDEA

Millions of different things can be made from a few building materials.

The ancient Greeks thought that everything is constructed from four elements—earth, air, fire, and water. Everything in the world would then be made by combining these four elements in different ways. In this view, people are made up of all four elements. We see evidence of this in the air entering and leaving our bodies, our heat (fire), our solid flesh and bones (earth), and our water parts (blood, sweat, tears). However, an ancient Greek named Dr. Artostotle failed when he tried to make a human being by adding 60 cups of water, 20 pots of soil, 10 breaths of air, and 2 bonfires.

According to the Greeks, the four elements themselves were the only things that are pure. Everything else was made by combining two or more of these elements in just the right way. The Greek idea of an element has two related parts:

> *Everything is made of elements. If we take anything and can break it down, we will find it is made of one or more of the four elements.*

> *We cannot break any of these four elements into something different.*

Greek Definition of Elements

Although we do not recognize the same four elements, modern science has followed the same approach as that used by the ancient Greeks. Instead of four elements, we have discovered that 92 elements naturally occur on our planet. All the millions of different kinds of Earth things are made by combining these 92 elements in different ways.

Water, one of the Greek Four, can help us understand why science has increased the number from four to 92. If water were an element, it could not be broken down into simpler elements. Yet, scientists discovered that water can be broken down fairly easily into two simpler building blocks.

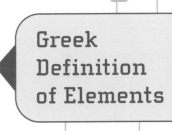

Water is not an element. It is made of hydrogen and oxygen.

Air is a mixture of nitrogen, oxygen, water, and carbon dioxide.

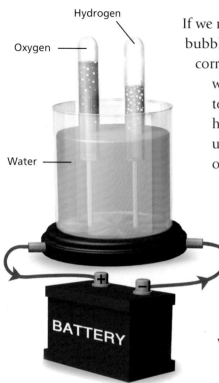

Hydrogen

Oxygen

Water

Water is not an element. It can be broken down into simpler building blocks

If we run an electric current through water, we can observe gas bubbles forming and escaping. If we set up our experiment correctly, we can collect two different gases coming from the water as it breaks down. By combining these two gases back together, we can make water. These gases are the elements hydrogen and oxygen. We call them elements because, unlike water, there is no easy way to break either hydrogen or oxygen into simpler building blocks.

Imagine that you own a company that has the job of constructing a planet such as Earth. At first, that seems an impossible job. You would need to keep a supply of all the millions of different kinds of things. However, now you know that the task is not so impossible. In theory, you would need only 92 different storage containers for your building materials. Whenever you needed anything like a rock or leaf or tooth, you could just gather the specific elements that make up that object, and put those elements together in exactly the right way.

It turns out that your job will be even easier than that. Most of the things on or in planet Earth are made from just a few elements. You will need large amounts of a few elements such as hydrogen, oxygen, carbon, nitrogen, iron, and silicon. They help make up water, soil, air, and living organisms. You will need smaller amounts of other elements such as aluminum, sulfur, and chlorine. For many elements, such as platinum and helium, your containers can be much smaller. These elements are present in very small quantities on Earth.

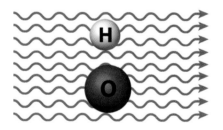

There is no easy way to break hydrogen or oxygen into simpler building blocks.

Our Awesome Systems Idea helps us understand why this works. The 92 elements are the parts of the Earth system. When two or more of these elements combine, they form new whole things that have different properties than the parts. Imagine all the ways you could combine 92 different things. No wonder we can have millions of different kinds of things on our planet.

Look how far we have already come in understanding the nature of things. Instead of needing to figure out how millions of different kinds of things are made, we have to deal with only 92 elements. You might think that is all we need to know, but science usually has another question up its sleeve.

What makes these elements different from each other? The answer to this question came as a result of investigations into the smallest possible pieces of an element. Democritus, one of those Greek thinkers, gave us the word that we use today for these smallest possible pieces of an element. Not only did we get a new word, we also reached a much deeper understanding of elements.

Atoms

Let's start by taking the Greek definition of an element and updating it. The idea of an element still has two parts:

Everything is made of elements. If we take anything and can break it down, we will find it is made of one or more of the 92 elements.

We cannot break any of these 92 elements into something different.

Updated Greek Definition of Elements

What happens when we try to break down an element? Gold is a particularly good example. You can take a piece of gold and heat it so much that it melts. That liquid stuff still behaves just like gold. You

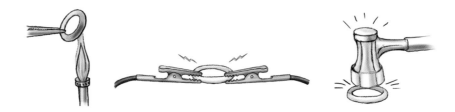

can run huge amounts of electricity through a piece of gold, and it will still behave just like gold. You can pound it incredibly thin, and it still behaves just like gold.

This dome was completely covered using less than an ounce of gold.

As one example, the dome of the Wyoming State Capitol Building is covered in gold leaf. The area of this dome is 800 square feet, and yet it took less than an ounce of gold to cover it. This is possible because gold leaf is extremely thin (about 0.00005 of an inch). It would take 20,000 pieces of gold leaf piled one on top of the other to have a piece one inch thick. Yet, this incredibly thin gold leaf still has the color, brilliance, and strength of gold. It is still gold.

So, how small could we cut a piece of gold? It turns out that there is a limit to how small something can be and still be gold. If you cut the gold leaf 10,000 times thinner, until it is only about 0.000000005 inches (0.000000013 centimeters) wide, you will have the smallest possible piece of material that still is gold. We call that very smallest piece an **atom** of gold.

An atom is incredibly small. Only recently have we been able to take pictures of atoms using very powerful microscopes. Cobalt is a metallic element, with magnetic properties similar to iron. The photo shows cobalt atoms (blue) against a copper background.

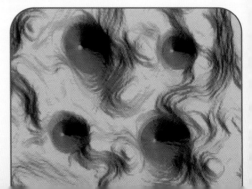

You can try the following exercise to get an idea of the atom's size. Take a sheet of paper that is 28 cm long by 2.5 cm wide. Cut it in half. Throw away one half, and cut the remaining piece in half. Keep doing this until you can no longer cut the paper in half. To get to the size of an atom, you would have to cut the paper about 20 more times.

We can now expand our definition of an element to say that it consists of atoms. The smallest piece of an element that you can see has gazillions of atoms of that element. Each of those atoms is essentially the same as every other atom of that element.

STOP AND THINK! There is another science question hiding up the sleeve of this description of elements and atoms.

What might that question be? Write it down; also write what you think the answer might be to that question. (Hint: if you are not sure about the question, read the three paragraphs beginning with, "So, how small can we cut a piece of gold?")

One way to ask that science question is: "What happens if we cut the atom into pieces?" I have written that the smallest possible piece of an element is an atom of that element. Can we break an atom? If yes, what happens?

It takes an incredibly huge amount of energy, but, yes, atoms can be broken. When we break an atom of gold, it stops being an atom of gold. If we could break it up into all its pieces and then separate those pieces, we would have different pieces that we call **subatomic particles**. "Subatomic" means smaller than an atom, and "particle" is another word for pieces.

The same results happen with other elements. If we break an atom of an element, it stops being that element. We get the same subatomic particles by breaking any element.

Now I can share with you an improved definition of an element. The idea of an element now has three parts:

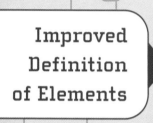

Improved Definition of Elements

> *Everything is made of elements. If we take anything and can break it down, we will find it is made of one or more of the 92 elements.*
>
> *Any piece of an element is made up of atoms of that element. Each of those atoms is essentially the same as every other atom of that element.*
>
> *We can break an atom of an element into subatomic particles. When we do that, it no longer is that element.*

Note that our definition includes two changes. It includes the new idea of atoms. It also says that we can break an element into pieces so small that it no longer is that element.

Atoms Are Systems

We can break an atom into parts. Therefore, atoms are systems. Each atom is an organized whole that is made of parts.

I will now share with you my favorite way to understand a system. Take the system, and add water. Shake rapidly side-to-side for fifteen minutes. That is, you shake rapidly from side to side, not the system. Leave the system alone. Lie down and rest; think about what you have learned.

If that does not work (which, I have to admit, is most of the time), I use a method that works much better. In this method, I ask and try to answer three questions about the system. No matter what the system is,

I can always understand it better by asking and trying to answer these three systems questions:

> *What are the parts of the system?*
>
> *How does the system work as a whole?*
>
> *How is the system itself part of larger systems?*

In this book, you will experience lots of examples where we get to understand a system by asking and answering these three systems questions.

By starting with the first systems question, we can answer a question so big that it cannot hide up the science sleeve. Why are the elements different from each other?

Oxygen

Since elements are made of atoms, it probably has something to do with the atoms. But what makes one atom different from another atom? Why is one atom hydrogen, while another atom is oxygen or gold?

Carbon

Gold

Why is one atom gold, while another atom is carbon, and a third is oxygen?

Parts Of The Atom

Here comes systems question #1: What are the parts of the atom? I have told you that atoms can be broken into subatomic particles.

THREE SUBATOMIC PARTICLES			
Particle	Size	Electric Charge	Effect of Adding or Removing
PROTON	"Big"	+1	Adding or removing protons changes the element into another element.
ELECTRON	"Tiny"	-1	The element stays the same after adding or removing electrons, but its electric charge changes.
NEUTRON	"Big"	0	The element type stays the same after adding or removing neutrons, but its weight changes. The atom may become more or less stable.

Many different subatomic particles exist, but we need to pay attention only to the three main ones. When we break an element into pieces, the three main pieces that we get are called protons, electrons, and neutrons.

As shown in the Table, the three subatomic particles differ in their size and electrical charge. Compared to the electron, both the proton and the neutron are big. Of course, since they are smaller than the atom, they really are not big. The proton and the neutron are about the same size, having 2,000 times the mass of an electron. The proton and electron have opposite electrical charges, which are called +1 and –1. The neutron has an electric charge of zero.

The last column gives us the answer to our question about what makes one element different from another element. This column compares what happens when we add or take away the different subatomic particles from an atom of an element. If we change the number of protons, we change the atom into another element. This major change does not happen when we change the number of electrons or neutrons.

Consider oxygen as an example. If we add two protons to an oxygen atom, it changes from oxygen to neon! We can use neon in an advertising light, but if we want a gas for breathing, pick oxygen over neon every time. This is a major change. Changing the number of protons changes an atom from being one kind of element into being another kind of element. The number of protons makes each element different from each other.

What happens if we add two electrons to an oxygen atom? It remains oxygen, but now the oxygen atom has an electric charge of minus two. This electric charge will change some features of how it behaves, but it remains oxygen.

7	8
N	O
Nitrogen	Oxygen

BIG IDEA

The number of protons makes each element different from one another.

What happens if we add two neutrons to an oxygen atom? It remains oxygen, but now the oxygen atom has somewhat more mass than it had before. Adding extra mass can make an atom more stable or less stable. In the case of oxygen, adding two neutrons makes it less stable, and it becomes radioactive.

Hydrogen, the simplest element, has only one proton. Helium has two protons, carbon six, nitrogen seven, oxygen eight, neon ten, gold 79, and uranium, the largest natural element, 92. Every hydrogen atom has one proton, every oxygen atom has eight protons, and every uranium atom has 92 protons.

Now that we know about subatomic particles, I can finally share with you the modern definition of an element. This definition still has three parts.

Modern Definition of Elements

> *Everything is made of elements. If we take anything and can break it down, we will find it is made of one or more of the 92 elements.*
>
> *Any piece of an element is made up of atoms of that element. Each of those atoms has the same number of protons.*
>
> *If we change the number of protons, we change an atom from being one element into being a different element.*

In this modern definition, we emphasize that elements are different from each other because the atoms of the elements have different numbers of protons.

Atoms As A Whole

Remember we are using Dr. Art's three systems questions to understand atoms. Answering the first question about the parts of the atom has helped us understand something that, in a way, makes you much smarter than the ancient Greeks.

Similarly, up until the 1800s many Europeans tried to change one element into another. They especially wanted to change lead into gold. They could never succeed because they did not know what you know about elements and subatomic particles. None of the methods they tried had any chance of changing the insides of atoms. These experimenters include some of the most famous scientists of their day, such as Sir Isaac Newton who discovered Newton's Laws of Motion, first explained how gravity works on Earth and in the solar system, and who also served as England's Master of the Royal Mint for 27 years. By knowing the parts of the atom, you cannot change lead into gold, but you know something about elements that Newton would have paid many gold coins to learn.

Our second systems question is: **How does the atom work as a whole?** The first thing to do in answering this question is to consider how the parts connect with each other to make the whole system.

By the year 1900, scientists knew that atoms had positive and negative electrical charges. They thought these charges were spread evenly throughout the atom. In 1908, a scientist from New Zealand named Ernest Rutherford decided to test that idea by shooting high-speed, positively charged particles at a thin sheet of gold foil.

Rutherford had two questions in mind: 1) What will happen when positively charged particles get shot at a thin sheet of gold foil? 2) What will this experiment tell us about the insides of atoms? He figured the positive particles would all pass right through the gold leaf because they were so big compared to anything inside the atom.

Detector

Atomic Particle Shooter

Gold Foil

Detector

However, Rutherford surprised himself and the rest of the scientific community when he discovered that some of his high-speed bullets came bouncing back at him from the gold foil. He often said that his results surprised him as much as if he had shot a cannon ball at tissue paper, and the cannon ball bounced back at him.

Rutherford had discovered what we call the atomic nucleus, the very tiny central region of the atom that has practically all the atom's mass. His experiments led to a model of the atom that we still use today. Those subatomic bullets had bounced back at him because they had hit the atomic nucleus. This nucleus occupies a very tiny fraction of the atom's space. The vast majority of Rutherford's subatomic bullets came nowhere near the nucleus so they passed right through the atom with little change in their path.

The Table of the three atomic particles now includes a column showing their location. Note that the massive protons and neutrons are located in the atom's nucleus. The tiny electrons are found in the outer edges of the atom.

THREE SUBATOMIC PARTICLES				
Particle	Location	Size	Electric Charge	Effect of Adding or Removing
PROTON	Nucleus	"Big"	+1	The element changes into another element.
ELECTRON	Outer edges	"Tiny"	-1	Element stays the same, but its electric charge changes.
NEUTRON	Nucleus	"Big"	0	Element stays the same, but its weight changes. Atom becomes more or less stable.

You may have seen drawings of atoms with electrons traveling in circles around a central nucleus. However, no drawing can accurately show you what the inside of an atom looks like. For one thing, it could never fit on a page or whiteboard or computer screen. Assume we use a marble to represent the nucleus of an atom. If we place the marble in the center of the Louisiana Superdome, then the electrons would be represented by wisps of dust waving for the home team from the outer edges of the structure.

The nucleus would be the size of a marble in the center, and electrons would be wisps of dust swirling on the outer edges.

The vast majority of the atom seems to be empty space. I hope you think that is weird. Everything that seems so solid to us is made of atoms that are mostly empty space. Unfortunately, in this chapter, I cannot help you understand how that could happen. You will have to wait until the next chapter.

Atoms As Part Of Larger Systems

Way back near the beginning of this chapter, I said that you could make a planet with just 92 containers, one for each of the different elements. These elements combine to make all the different things. Since the elements are made of atoms, the things that are combining are actually the atoms of the element.

For example, take water. Our most important liquid consists of two atoms of hydrogen combined with one atom of oxygen (abbreviated as H_2O). Hydrogen and oxygen can combine in another way to form hydrogen peroxide, a chemical that we use as a bleach and to kill bacteria. Hydrogen peroxide consists of two hydrogen atoms combined with two atoms of oxygen (abbreviated as H_2O_2).

The same two elements can combine to form very different things. We need water to live. Drinking pure hydrogen peroxide can kill you.

Water and hydrogen peroxide are both examples of a larger system that is made when two or more atoms combine with each other. They each have very different properties than the elements that are their parts (hydrogen atoms and oxygen atoms). Whenever two or more different elements combine with each other, we say that they form a compound. A compound will always have properties that are different than its parts.

When we cut gold into smaller and smaller pieces, we finally got a piece that was so small that if we cut it any more, it would no longer be gold. We gave the name "atom" to that smallest possible piece.

Hydrogen
Peroxide

What happens when we take water and keep dividing our sample into smaller and smaller volumes. We finally reach a size where we cannot make it any smaller. At that size, we have one thing that consists of two hydrogen atoms connected to one oxygen atom.

What should we call that smallest piece of water? We cannot call it an atom of water. We use the atom word only for elements. Water is a compound, not an element. Therefore, scientists have to use a new word to name the smallest piece of a compound. That name is molecule.

In the previous paragraph we defined a molecule as the smallest piece of a compound. Here is another definition that is a little more accurate. Whenever two or more atoms join together, they form a molecule. A molecule is the particle that is formed by two or more atoms joining together.

The simplest molecules consist of only two atoms joined together. The largest molecules can have hundreds of thousands of atoms joined together in a very precise way. Examples of these very large molecules are plastics, protein, DNA, and starch.

BIG DEFINITION

A molecule is the particle that is formed when two or more atoms join together.

Millions From Three

Our job to make planet Earth has become a lot easier. We do not need compartments for a million different things. To start, we do not even need 92 different things. We can make all the 92 different elements using just three building blocks. We just need to be able to store and put together the three different building blocks that we will use to make the 92 different elements. We will then combine those elements to make anything on our planet.

Here is a recipe for some of the elements we will want.

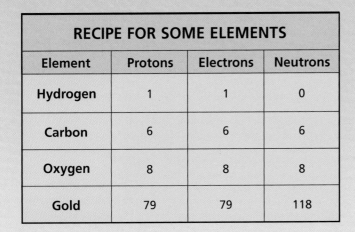

RECIPE FOR SOME ELEMENTS			
Element	Protons	Electrons	Neutrons
Hydrogen	1	1	0
Carbon	6	6	6
Oxygen	8	8	8
Gold	79	79	118

We certainly want water. First we make hydrogen by combining one proton and one electron. Next we make oxygen by combining eight protons, eight electrons, and eight neutrons. Then for each molecule of water, we combine two atoms of hydrogen with one atom of oxygen. We do that lots of times and we will have enough water to fill a glass. Let's drink a toast to matter! Cheers!

STOP & THINK

Some readers think that reading means correctly pronouncing the words. That is like saying that eating is mostly about chewing the food, and not about tasting it or getting nutrition. Yes, you have to chew the food. Yes, you have to know how to make the words from the letters and try to pronounce them correctly. But reading is about understanding (tasting) and growing because of what you learn (nutrition).

Good readers use lots of strategies to get the most understanding. They often are not even aware of the methods that they use as they read. You can become a better reader by becoming aware of the reading strategies you may already be using, and by learning and practicing new ones.

Like scientists, good readers ask and answer questions. You may already be doing this, but you may not be aware that you ask questions as you read. Asking and answering questions can be a very powerful strategy to help you understand what you are reading.

Let's look at a sentence from this chapter to illustrate what I mean. After I described Rutherford's experiment, I wrote: Rutherford had discovered what we call the atomic nucleus, the very tiny central region of the atom that has practically all the atom's mass.

If you had never heard of an atom's nucleus, part of your brain should be asking, "What does that word mean?" To answer that question, you would look at the rest of the paragraph to find out more about the nucleus and the inside structure of the atom. You could also look at the drawing of Rutherford's experiment to see if that showed where the nucleus is. You could also look in the Glindex on page 240 to see if that section has anything about the atomic nucleus.

As another example, when you read that Rutherford was surprised at his results, you could be asking yourself if you understand why he was so surprised. If the answer is no, then it means you probably should read about it again.

ENERGY
AND DR. ART's 50th ANNIVERSARY BALL

Chapter 4 – *Energy*
and Dr. Art's 50th Anniversary Ball

Exploring Energy

We can make a planet from 92 elements that combine to make all the solid, liquid, and gas stuff. However, if all we have are the 92 elements and their combinations, then hardly anything will happen. We could call the planet "Boring." Planet Boring does not include a key feature of our planet. Planet Boring does not have the **energy** for things to move around.

Without energy, we could not even make Planet Boring. We need energy to combine the elements into the millions of different kinds of things. We need energy to put those things into their correct locations.

So, what is energy? We use the word energy in our everyday language. If we see people racing or playing sports, we say they have lots of energy. We know that our homes and cars use lots of energy. We feel the energy from the Sun, and we experience that food gives us energy.

Energy is also a science word. In science, we can measure the amounts of energy in a scoop of ice cream, a hot pool, a gallon of gasoline, a hurricane, and an electric battery. With science, we can precisely measure how much energy a tiger uses when it runs.

Energy: hurricane approaching Florida.

Energy: Yellowstone hot pool, and hungry tiger.

While science can measure energy very, very precisely, it actually has a hard time defining the word. One official science definition states that energy is the ability to move matter. In this science definition, if you carry three heavy bags of groceries up a hill, you are moving matter and therefore using energy. However, if a cruel person makes you stand motionless for an hour holding the same three heavy bags, this science definition says you are not moving matter, and therefore not using any energy to hold the bags.

In this book, we are not going to learn the science meaning of energy by memorizing a definition. Instead, we will explore different science situations that involve energy. This is the way we learn the meaning of many words, especially those with deep meanings, such as energy or love.

How would you define love? Any definition would have to include the many different forms of love. For example, I love my family, but I feel different kinds of love for my wife, father, daughter, and brother. I also love sunsets, the Bob Marley reggae song "Wake Up And Live," friends, writing this book, hiking in a redwood forest, my tie-dyed lab coat, money, my bed, and the sound of birds singing. All these different examples help define the word love.

Just like love, energy is a complicated and important word. Back in the ancient days of the last century, the Beatles knew that. They wrote a very popular rock and roll song called, "All You Need Is Energy."

Forms of Energy

Planet Earth, unlike Planet Boring, features both matter and energy. Matter is the stuff of our world. Energy makes matter move, raises its temperature, melts solids, and boils liquids. Energy causes changes in matter.

Rub your hands together. Where did you get the energy to move your hands back and forth? It came from chemical energy stored in food. Remember photosynthesis from the first two chapters? That food chemical energy came from light energy from the Sun. For you to be able to rub your hands together, light energy from the Sun changed into chemical energy, which changed into motion energy.

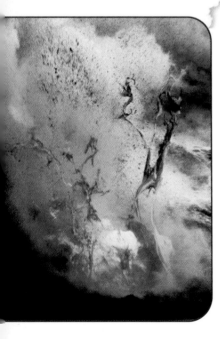

Energy causes changes in matter.

It took scientists a long time to figure out that light, motion, electricity, and heat all involve energy. Today we say that they are all forms of energy. We also say that energy readily changes from one form to another.

What happened when you rubbed your hands together? You experienced motion energy changing into heat energy. This phenomenon of motion changing to heat played a big role in helping scientists understand energy.

To investigate the different forms of energy, scientists measured how much heat energy they would get from a measured amount of motion energy. Benjamin Thompson, who became known as Count Rumford, performed one of the first experiments. Born in Massachusetts in 1753, he spied for the British during the American War of Independence. Revealed as a spy, he had to leave his wife and infant daughter, and flee to Europe to save his life.

While living in Europe, he continued spying for different countries, but he also did great science. Rumford invented efficient fireplaces, the first instrument to measure the amount of light, and the modern drip way to make coffee. He helped set up a system of housing and jobs for poor people, and he also designed efficient ways to organize armies.

During his work with armies, he investigated the heat created when a cannon is made by boring a hole into a big cylinder of iron. Count Rumford set up an experiment where a horse running in a circle turned a metal borer against a cannon. The cannon was totally covered with water. The friction heat of the borer grinding into the cannon raised the water's temperature. Count Rumford reported that the bystanders were astonished when three gallons of cold water were heated to boiling in this way without any fire.

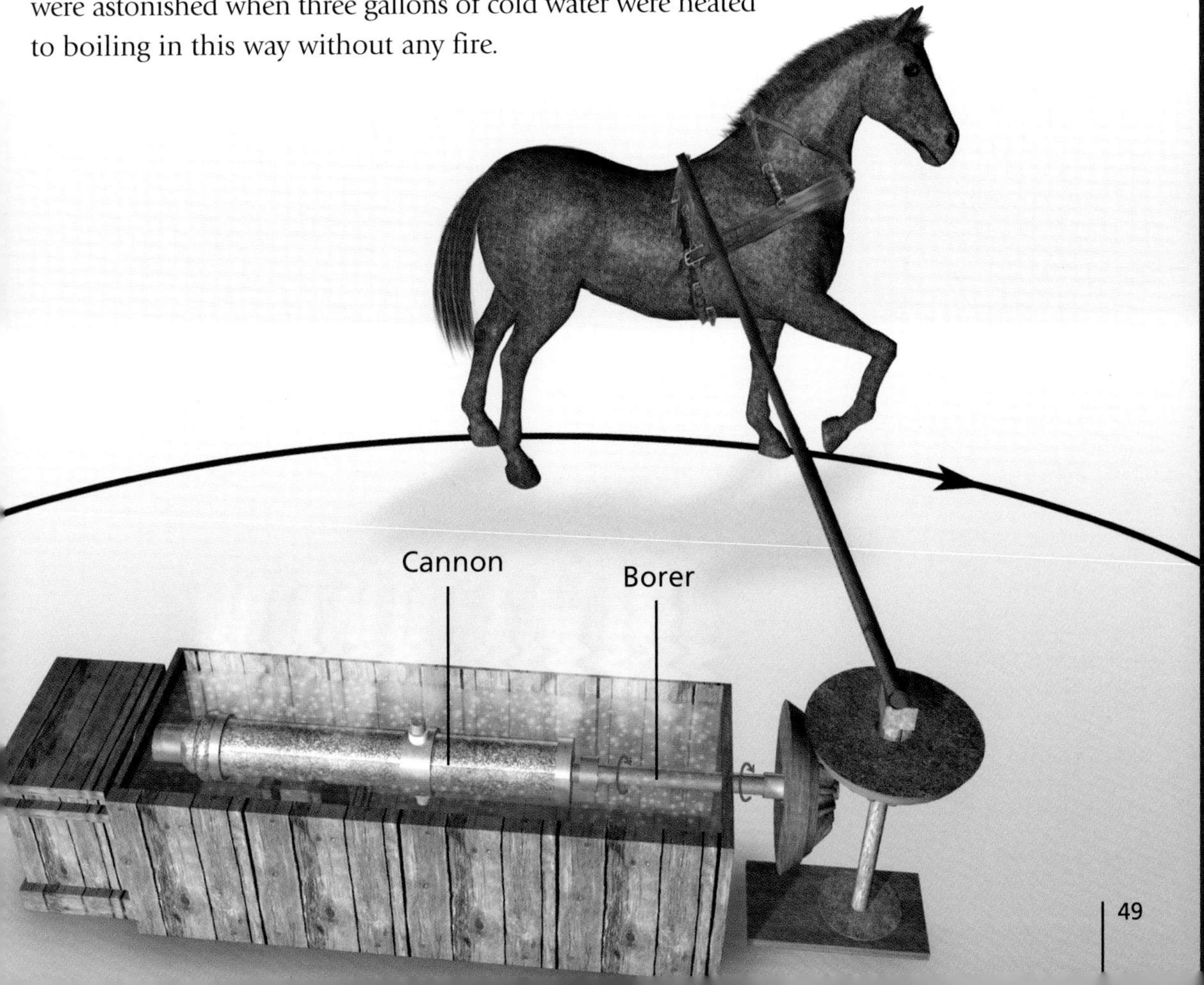

Cannon

Borer

Many experiments such as Rumford's proved that when energy changes forms, none of it disappears or gets created. This result became known as the **Law of Conservation of Energy**. This law states that energy is never created or destroyed. Whenever something happens, the amount of energy is exactly the same at the beginning as at the end.

At first sight, this scientific law does not fit our experience of the world. We fill a car's gas tank on Monday, drive 350 miles during the week, and then we have to put more gas in the tank on Sunday. Our local energy company charges us for the oil or natural gas that we use to heat our home. If we refuse to pay the bill and send a letter to the company arguing that scientific law tells us that we did not use up the energy, what do you think the answer will be?

The Law of Energy Conservation takes a much broader view of energy than we normally do. When we heat our home, we pay attention only to the fuel and the heat in the house. The Energy Conservation Law follows the heat after it leaves the house, watches it escape through the atmosphere, spread into outer space, and notices that the heat continues to exist forever—it is never destroyed. Further, the amount of heat energy exactly equals the amount of chemical energy released from the fuel (such as gas, oil or wood). The company bills us, but not because we destroy energy. We pay the electric and gas bill because we use up a particularly convenient form of stored energy, and change the energy into a form that is much less useful.

BIG IDEA

Energy always remains constant in amount. Energy is neither created nor destroyed.

Your Gas & Electric Co.
Anycity, USA

To: Dr. Art

Thank you for reminding us about the Law of Energy Conservation. Last month we supplied you with 200,000 units of energy that was contained in coal, oil and natural gas. That energy has probably already left our planet as heat. If you can capture it and package it in a convenient form, we will buy it back from you. Otherwise, forget it.

Sincerely,

V. Engy

N. Ergy, Customer Relations Department

Energy Of Motion

Movement is one of the most visible ways that we become aware of energy. Not only is visible motion a sign of energy, it turns out that invisible motion is equally, if not more, important.

Invisible motion? Is that one of those Dr. Art tricks? No, I am referring to movement at the atomic level of reality. In the previous chapter, we discussed that everything is made of atoms. These atoms combine to form molecules, such as a molecule of water, consisting of two hydrogen atoms and one oxygen atom bonded to each other. These atoms and molecules do not just hang around doing nothing.

The **atomic theory of matter** tells us that atoms and molecules constantly move and vibrate. The atoms within a water molecule vibrate and jiggle in their positions. Each molecule also moves, constantly banging into other water molecules.

In some conditions, water molecules make fairly strong connections with each other. They move around much less, and they tend to stay with the same neighboring water molecules. They still jiggle around within those locations, but they don't change from one location to another. We have a name for this kind of water—ice.

In a solid, such as ice, the individual molecules connect fairly strongly with each other. They resist being separated. That is why a solid block of ice will keep its shape even if you put it in a bigger container.

This feature of solids begins to answer the question about why matter can feel so solid even though atoms are mostly empty space. When we push on a solid, the molecules resist being separated. They hold onto each other. Physicists (scientists who specialize in matter, energy, and forces) would say that the molecules hold on to each other so strongly that they even push back at us.

Here is my favorite way to describe the differences between solids, liquids, and gases. Imagine a huge party called Dr. Art's 50th Anniversary Ball. Everybody there is part of a couple that is celebrating their 50th wedding anniversary.

In the first dance, the DJ makes all the couples stand next to each other, occupying only a quarter of the dance floor. She ties two ribbons on each person's back. The 50-year partners hug each other in a formal, old-fashioned, dancing position. Each person also firmly holds in his or her mouth two ribbons, one from each of two different neighbors. In this way, each person is tightly connected to the spouse, and less tightly connected to two neighboring people.

The music starts and the DJ puts on a really slow song. Each couple moves, but the ribbons make them keep more or less in the same position, with the same neighbors. They all move, but the whole group keeps the same shape.

At the end of the song, the DJ announces that they have just done the Dr. Art Solid Dance. Each person represents an atom. By hugging each other in dance position, they model how two atoms bind tightly to each other to form a molecule. In this way, each couple represents a molecule made of two atoms. The ribbons represent the ways that each molecule connects with its neighboring molecules in a solid.

When we push on a solid, the molecules resist being separated. They hold onto each other.

The dancers protest to the DJ that they did not come to Dr. Art's 50th Anniversary Ball so they could jiggle in one spot in the room. She does not understand what they are saying because they all have ribbons in their mouths. She tells them to take the ribbons out of their mouths. She also tells them that they can now move around and have different neighbors. They still cannot change partners, and they have to stay on the dance floor.

She puts on the song "Old Man River." As before, the couples remain attached to each other, but now they flow around the dance floor, changing who their neighbors are. As they bang into another couple, they grab a ribbon, hold onto it, and then let it go. In this way, they keep changing who their neighbors are, but they more or less stay together as a group. The DJ adds a new section of dance floor, and couples immediately fill that space as well.

At the end of the song, the DJ announces that they have just done the Dr. Art Liquid Dance. Like a liquid, the whole group easily changes its shape. Unlike a solid, the group of molecules can flow and adjust to the shape of the container. Compared with the solid, the individual molecules in a liquid are less connected with each other and less locked in place.

Now the DJ cuts off the ribbons and throws them away. She tells the couples that they have to move as fast as they can all around the ballroom. However, each couple still has to stay tightly connected. The food tables and chairs have all been removed. She puts on the Rolling Stones song, "Jumping Jack Flash. It's A Gas! Gas! Gas!" When the couples bang into each other, they just bounce off each other, and keep on boogying. You know what Dr. Art Dance they are doing. Like a gas, they fill all the space in the container, and, as a group, they take whatever shape their container provides.

The senior citizen couples have asked for a rest, so we are taking a short break from the Dr. Art 50th Anniversary Ball. While they catch their breath, I want to make sure you realize that by changing each dance, the DJ modeled a change from a solid to a liquid to a gas. At the Ball, the change happened because the DJ gave instructions. In the real world, these kinds of changes happen because more energy is added, causing the molecules to become more active and less attached to each other. On our level of reality, we use the words melting and evaporating to describe what we see when these changes happen at the molecular level.

In science classes, we use the phrase "physical changes" to describe melting, freezing, evaporating, and condensing. These changes happen when energy is added to a system and it becomes hotter (melting, evaporating) or when energy leaves a system and it becomes colder (condensing, freezing).

One important take-home message is that:

HEAT = Energy of Motion of Molecules and Atoms

When we add energy to any material, its molecules will move and jiggle faster. If we take energy away from any material, its molecules will move and jiggle slower. If we see molecules slowing down in their motions, we know they have less heat energy. If we see molecules beginning to move faster, we know they have more heat energy.

Hold everything! A news flash has just arrived from the Ball!

Chemical Energy

A revolt is happening on the dance floor. The DJ has told the couples that they have to change partners. They scream, "We came here to celebrate our marriage as couples. We are tightly bonded to each other. If we break those bonds and connect with other people, we will become totally different!"

The DJ shows no mercy. Professional wrestlers separate the husbands and wives from each other. The wrestlers then join these individuals to strangers, making them hold each other in groups of different sizes, not just couples. There are groups with three members, eight members, and even one group with 27 members. The DJ tells them they are doing the Dr. Art Chemical Changes Dance, and puts on the 1950s Golden Oldie, "Breaking Up Is Hard To Do."

While this is a very sad story, I had to tell it because it shows the differences between physical changes and chemical changes. In a **physical change**, such as melting or evaporating, the molecules stay the same. Water remains H_2O in the solid, liquid, and gas states. In a **chemical change**, the atoms bind to different atoms. The molecules themselves change.

> In a chemical change, the atoms bind to different atoms. The molecules themselves change.

Photosynthesis provides an example of a chemical change. When water combines with carbon dioxide to make sugar, each water molecule is torn apart. The hydrogen atoms that were connected to the oxygen atom in water break that bond, and connect instead with oxygen atoms in carbon dioxide. The water molecules and the carbon dioxide molecules disappear.

In general, atoms within molecules bind to each other much more tightly than the ways that one molecule will connect with another molecule. In the Ball, the DJ could easily get the couples to change how they interacted with other couples. In contrast, she needed professional wrestlers to break the couples apart.

The Ball also shows that physical changes do not change the identity of the molecules. The couples remain the same. With chemical changes, the atoms connect with different atoms, and they become entirely new systems (new molecules) with qualitatively different properties.

Chemical changes happen inside us and all around us. Check out the examples below.

Familiar Examples Of Chemical Changes

- *Any fire that you see (gas stove, fireplace)*

- *Digesting the food you eat into molecules small enough for your body to use*

- *Any vehicle that uses fossil fuels (car, bus, plane)*

- *Any time you move a muscle in your body (for example, to breathe, walk, talk), or sense your environment (see, smell, taste, hear, touch).*

Chemical changes usually involve changes in energy. We tend to take advantage of chemical changes that give off energy. For example, when we burn a piece of wood or a gallon of gasoline, the wood molecules or gasoline molecules combine with oxygen to form carbon dioxide. Those chemical changes release energy that we experience as heat and light. Our vehicles convert this released energy into motion energy to carry us from place to place.

Chemical changes do not create energy. If they did, they would violate the Law of Conservation of Energy, and they would be locked up in jail. So, how can we get energy from burning anything, such as a piece of wood?

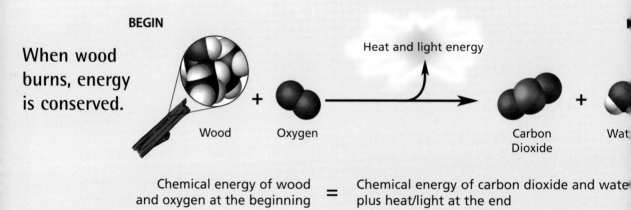

BEGIN

When wood burns, energy is conserved.

Wood + Oxygen

Heat and light energy

Carbon Dioxide + Wat

Chemical energy of wood and oxygen at the beginning = Chemical energy of carbon dioxide and wate plus heat/light at the end

The answer involves knowing that every molecule has chemical energy. Some molecules have more chemical energy than others. If we add up the chemical energy in the molecules, we discover how we can get energy from burning fuels, and not get locked in prison for breaking the Law.

The illustration shows how the process of burning a piece of wood obeys the Conservation Law. When wood burns, wood molecules combine with oxygen molecules to form carbon dioxide molecules and water molecules. The chemical energy of the beginning molecules (wood and oxygen) is greater than the chemical energy of the molecules at the end (carbon dioxide and water). This extra chemical energy is released as heat and light energy.

Energy is conserved. The total amount of energy at the end (chemical energy of carbon dioxide and water *plus heat/light energy*) is the same as the total energy at the beginning (chemical energy of wood and oxygen).

Why Matter Is Hard

The DJ announces that the time has come to do the Dr. Art Nuclear Changes Dance. All the people, including the wrestlers, run out of the building as fast as they can. That's a shame. I had planned to use this dance to explain nuclear energy. Now we will have to wait until Chapter 6 to discuss nuclear energy.

On the bright side, we can take this opportunity to answer the question that we raised in the last chapter. Why do we experience matter (including ourselves!) as being solid when atoms are so empty? Are we really that holey?

A major part of the answer is that molecules connect with each other. In a solid, the molecules connect so tightly with each other that they resist being separated. We feel this strong resistance, and call the substance a "solid." In some solids, such as butter, the molecules do not hold each quite so strongly. We experience that kind of material as being a soft, slippery solid.

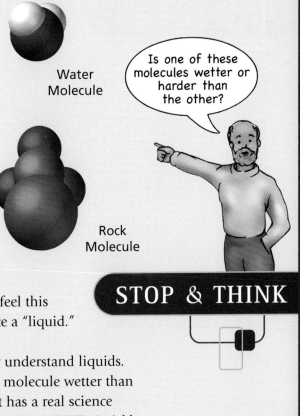

Water Molecule

Rock Molecule

Is one of these molecules wetter or harder than the other?

STOP & THINK

In a liquid, the molecules connect even less tightly with each other. We can dip a finger into a liquid. The water molecules move apart, and flow around the finger. But they still stick together to flow as a whole. We feel this kind of weaker resistance, and call the substance a "liquid."

Let's **STOP AND THINK** to make sure we truly understand liquids. Think about the following question: Is a water molecule wetter than a rock molecule? This is not a trick question. It has a real science answer. Better than "stop and think," try **STOP AND WRITE**. Quickly take a piece of paper, and write at least two sentences saying whether you think a water molecule is wetter than a rock molecule or not, and include at least one reason why you gave that answer.

✎ *Time To Stop & Write Now* ✎

Most of you have probably been feeling frustrated that we have hardly used our favorite science word in this chapter. Have no fear. Systems are here. Here is a clue for answering the question: think about a liquid as a system. You might want to change or add to what you already wrote.

My science answer is that a water molecule is not wetter than a rock molecule. Similarly, a rock molecule is not harder than a water molecule. An individual molecule is neither hard, nor wet, nor dry, nor soft. There have to be lots of molecules interacting with each other before those properties exist. Wetness and hardness are properties of systems of molecules, not of individual molecules.

BIG IDEA

We are systems of molecules that experience other systems of molecules.

One water molecule is not wet. Three water molecules are not wet. I don't know the minimum number of water molecules to create "wetness." I do know that it takes gazillions of molecules before we can become aware of wetness or hardness on our level of reality. The smallest drop of water that we can see consists of more than 10,000,000,000,000,000,000,000 (ten thousand billion billion) water molecules.

We experience systems of immense numbers of molecules that have properties (such as wetness or hardness) that the individual molecules do not have. As the Awesome Systems Idea tells us, a system has properties that are qualitatively different than those of the parts.

We are systems of molecules that experience other systems of molecules. Matter appears hard to us because the experiencing system (us) and the object that we experience both are made of gazillions of connected molecules. The experience of wetness or hardness is a systems experience.

STOP & THINK

When you read something that has a lot of information, it helps to use reading strategies to make sure you understand the most important information. One method is to look over the chapter, and summarize in your own words the main ideas.

Try that. Look over Chapter 4. Pick out the ideas that you think are most important. Write them using your own words. Keep it short and simple, less than a page long.

After you do that, compare what you wrote with the summary shown on the next page in red. I hired a professional summarizer, and this is what she wrote. See what you both included. Compare things that you wrote that she did not, and vice versa.

Professional Summary of Chapter 4

Energy causes changes in matter. It makes matter move, increases its temperature, melts it, and can even boil it. It exists in many different forms such as motion energy, chemical energy, electrical energy, and light energy.

Atoms and molecules constantly vibrate and jiggle. What we experience as heat is the energy of motion of molecules and atoms. The hotter something is, the more its molecules and atoms move and vibrate.

Energy easily changes from one form to another. Whenever anything happens, the total amount of energy remains the same. Energy is neither created nor destroyed. This is called the Law of Conservation of Energy.

Solids, liquids, and gases are different because the molecules in those substances move differently. The molecules in solids are kind of locked in place, and keep the same neighbors. In liquids, the molecules connect with their neighbors but not as tightly as in solids. That is why liquids can flow and change shape. In gases, the molecules move much faster and do not connect with their neighbors.

The connections between atoms within a molecule are much stronger than the connections between one molecule and another molecule. It is much harder to separate these atoms from each other than to separate molecules from each other.

Chemical reactions, such as burning, often give off energy. That happens when the products have less chemical energy than the starting materials.

Matter feels solid to us because we experience the connections among the molecules. Also the feeling of solidness or wetness is a systems property. The individual molecules are not wet or dry or solid or soft. We are systems of molecules that experience other systems of molecules.

www.guidetoscience.net

FORCES BE WITH US

Chapter 5 – Forces Be With Us

Gravity Is Universal

As you can tell from the title, this chapter focuses on forces. Heroes in the Star Wars movies trained all their lives so "The Force" could be with them. Few people know that Yoda, the ancient Jedi master, visited England in 1687 to learn the science of forces from Isaac Newton.

Like the words "energy" and "theory," "force" is another word that people commonly use, and that scientists use in ways that differ from the common language meanings. In science, "force" does not have the supernatural Jedi warrior meaning. However, you will discover that science warriors who investigate forces explore mysterious levels of reality.

To understand forces, it helps to know about matter and energy. Fortunately, you have memorized Chapters 3 and 4, so you know a lot about matter and energy.

One way that scientists investigate forces is to observe matter and how it moves in the world. Whenever anything (matter) changes its motion (energy), we know that a force has acted upon it. The change in motion could be that the object stops moving, begins moving, changes directions, speeds up, or slows down.

When an apple falls from a tree, we know that a force must have acted on that apple. A person who catches the apple feels the force of the falling object. In catching it, the person also exerts a force on the object to stop its downward motion.

For as long as humans have lived on this planet, we have seen objects, such as fruit and leaves, falling to the ground. Galileo, the guy who first saw the moons of Jupiter, was also the first person to scientifically measure the force that pulls objects downward. He measured how fast things moved when he rolled balls down ramps, or when he dropped feathers and other objects from towers.

At the same time, Galileo and other scientists were also investigating how planets and moons travel in the solar system. They even had complicated math equations that predicted where any planet would be on a particular date, and the exact path it would continue traveling.

Newton was a genius. Where everybody else saw things falling to the ground, he saw one of the most important ways that matter interacts throughout the universe. Newton discovered gravity. He realized that every object attracts every other object via gravity. Whenever you use or hear the word gravity, it is because Isaac Newton first understood it and gave it the modern scientific meaning.

The same force causes apples to fall from trees and the Moon to travel around Earth.

Newton and Yoda sat under an apple tree and talked about gravity. According to rumor, Newton saw an apple fall from a tree while the Moon was shining, and he realized that the same force causes apples to fall from trees and the Moon to travel around Earth. Earth and an apple attract each other because they both have mass. (For now, think of mass simply as the amount of matter.) Since Earth has way more mass than the apple, the fruit falls to the ground.

Newton realized that the Moon and Earth also attract each other. The Moon keeps circling Earth because the mass of our planet constantly pulls it in. The same kind of thing happens when you swing a ball on a string. The ball moves in a circle because the string constantly pulls it toward your hand. In the case of orbiting moons or planets, gravity is the force that pulls inward.

To prove that the same gravity works on Earth and in the heavens, Newton had to invent a brand new field of mathematics to exactly calculate the strength of attraction between objects,[1] and how that attraction causes the motions that we see. His math accurately described the motions of moons, planets, and objects, such as apples and balls, falling to the ground.

Newton's work resulted in equations that have become known as Newton's Law of Gravitational Attraction and Newton's Laws of Motion. Newton's mathematics teaches us that the force of gravity between two objects depends on their mass and on the distance separating them. The more mass they have, the greater the force of gravity attracting them to each other. The further apart they are, the weaker is the force of gravity attracting them to each other.

Newton taught us that the same science explains how things work on our planet and in the heavens. Previously, people had thought that heavenly bodies did not obey the same physical laws as those on Earth. Now we know that the same science applies in the same way throughout the universe.

If we learn something about how X-rays are produced by observing them traveling here from the farthest reaches of space, those discoveries will apply to X-rays here on Earth. If we discover that hydrogen behaves a certain way on planet Earth, we can expect that under the same conditions, it will have the same properties in the Sun and in other stars, no matter how far away they are from us.

The same science ...

BIG IDEA

... applies throughout the universe.

---

[1] That field of mathematics is called *calculus*. More than 300 years after Newton, many engineers and scientists still use calculus in their work.

Newton became very famous for his science that teaches us about gravity and the rules governing how everything moves. However, he remained puzzled about how these forces work. If two objects are distant from each other, they are not physically touching. If I throw an apple, I understand that my physical action makes it move. But how does Earth affect the motion of an apple, or of the Moon, when it does not physically touch those objects?

Newton told Yoda that this "action at a distance" made gravity seem as mysterious as Yoda's "Force." In the next section, we will explore another force that has the same spooky ability to invisibly travel across space and affect the way things move.

Stronger Than Gravity

This section has the title, "Stronger Than Gravity." The force of gravity from the Sun holds all the solar system's planets in their orbits. Earth's force of gravity holds the Moon, and prevents it from flying into the Sun. What could be stronger than a force that holds entire planets and moons in their positions?

You can directly experience this "stronger than gravity" force. Simply cut a small piece of paper into pieces that are about 1 cm by 1 cm in length, and spread the pieces on a table. Take a balloon and blow it up with air. Rub the balloon hard and often with a piece of fur, wool, or cotton. Now bring the balloon close to the paper. You should see some pieces of paper jump up to and stick to the balloon. (This experiment works best on dry days. If conditions are humid or wet, experiments involving static electricity may not work.)

You can also sprinkle some uncoated, metallic paper clips on the table. Hold a magnet over the clips. Even with a small magnet, you may be able to lift ten paper clips.

In both cases, the entire gravity of planet Earth was pulling on the objects to keep them on the table. The **static electric force** exerted by the balloon overpowered all of Earth's gravity to pick up the paper. The **magnetic force** exerted by the small magnet also proved stronger than the gravitational attraction of all of Earth's matter.

Both electricity and magnetism are much stronger than gravity. They also feature the same "action at a distance" as gravity. Gravity only attracts, while both magnetism and electricity can cause repulsion (pushing away) as well as attraction. Depending on how you arrange two magnets, they will either attract or repel each other. We call one side or end of the magnet a north pole and the other a south pole. Opposite poles attract each other, and the same magnetic poles push each other away.

Electricity shows a similar property. Something can be positively charged (for example, the proton) or negatively charged (for example, the electron). Things that have opposite electrical charge attract each other, and things that have the same electrical charge push each other away. You can experience electrical repulsion by rubbing two inflated balloons with the same material (wool or fur work best). If you hang each balloon from a string and, holding just the string, carefully bring them next to each other, you will see that the balloons push each other away.

Why do the two rubbed balloons repel each other? When we rub a balloon with material such as wool or fur, we actually rub some of the electrons off the material onto the rubber surface of the balloon. As a result, the extra electrons on the surface of the

balloon make it negatively charged. Since we rubbed each balloon
the same way, they will both be negatively charged. If we bring them
close together, they will push each other away.

The explanation why the rubbed balloon will pick up pieces
of paper is a little more complicated. Like most matter,
the pieces of paper are electrically neutral.
Everywhere in the paper the number
of protons (positive charge) is
equal to the number of electrons
(negative charge), so the
total charge is zero. When
we bring a negatively
charged balloon close to
the paper, its extra negative charges
cause the electrons on the surface of
the paper to move away. That makes
the nearby part of the paper become
positively charged because the
negative electrons have left the
area. This positively charged surface
of the paper is then attracted to the
negatively charged balloon, and
the paper jumps off the table due to
the attraction between opposite
electric charges.

Surface paper atoms
with uniform electron
distribution.

Extra electrons on
surface of balloon.

Surface paper atoms
with distorted
electron distribution.

In the next section, we will do some experiments that show that
electricity and magnetism are actually part of the same force. Scientists
call this force **electromagnetism**. As we saw with the balloons and
the magnets, electromagnetism is much stronger than gravity.
Physicists generally say that electromagnetism is millions of times
stronger than gravity.

Electricity Plus Magnetism Equals ?

We experience electricity through the wires in our homes that power our lights, refrigerators, televisions, blenders, hair dryers, heaters, and computers. In that wiring, we take advantage of the fact that electrons in metals can move very easily. Because metals conduct electricity so well, we make our wires out of copper and aluminum. These metal wires enable electrons to flow from power stations to and through our home wiring. This guided flow of electrons powers our electrical devices.

We also experience electricity in batteries. They store electrical charge that can then provide power to a wide variety of devices. Batteries work by pushing electrons from one end of the battery through our tools and toys (such as a cell phone) and back into the other end of the battery.

We also experience static electricity when fluff sticks to our clothes or a spark shocks us by jumping between our hand and a door knob. We can also move electrons around by rubbing balloons with cloth, and then use those balloons in science experiments to repel each other or pick up pieces of paper.

BIG IDEA

Electricity is built into matter.

Home wiring, batteries, and static electricity all reveal something very deep about the nature of matter. They help us understand that electricity is built into matter. Electrons are not just a word that we read in science books. Everything is made of atoms, and these atoms consist of electrically charged pieces, the negatively charged electrons and the positively charged protons. Matter has an electrical basis. Batteries and home wiring are just a few, very specialized forms of electricity where we have learned how to take advantage of the fact that electricity is built into all matter.

have learned how to take advantage of the fact that electricity is built into all matter.

The same lesson holds true for magnetism. We mostly experience magnetism through toys and tools in our homes. Actually, magnetism is very closely related to electricity. Magnetism is way more important than cute objects sticking to refrigerator doors.

People usually first learn that electricity and magnetism are related when they learn about electromagnets. In this section, I am going to describe some experiments that you can try. The supplies you will need for the next two experiments are:

- 4 meters (12 feet) of 20 gauge, copper, insulated, stranded hook-up wire;
- an iron nail at least 15 centimeters (cm) long
- a good 1.5 volt D-size battery
- five round ceramic magnets (1 1/8 inch diameter is a good size)

INSTRUCTIONS: Cut off 30 cm (centimeters) of the wire and put it aside. With the longer piece, remove the insulation from each end for about 2 cm of the wire. Leave about 30 cm of one end loose, and then wrap the wire around the nail. Start at the wide end and keep winding tightly in circles down the nail in the same direction. Avoid overlapping the wire. When you reach the other end,

Before you connect it to the battery, test if your wrapped nail will pick up uncoated metallic paper clips. Test both ends of the nail. Take a round ceramic magnet and mark one side as Side A, and the other side as Side B. Now, test to see if the two ends of the nail behave the same or differently with the two poles (sides) of a round ceramic magnet. Write down your results using a Table like the one below.

Now, connect one end of the wire to the positive top of the 1.5 volt battery, and the other end of the wire to the negative bottom of the battery. You can do this with tape or with a battery holder. Check both ends of the nail to see if it can pick up any of the paper clips. Also, test each end of the nail with the two different sides of the round magnet. Disconnect the wires from the battery (or you will quickly drain its power)! After a minute, check again how the wire interacts with the paper clips and the round magnet. Write your results, and compare with and without the battery.

Electromagnet Experiment			
STATUS	ACTION	BLUNT END OF NAIL	SHARP END OF NAIL
NOT CONNECTED	Picks up paper clip		
	Interaction with Side A		
	Interaction with Side B		
CONNECTED TO BATTERY	Picks up paper clip		
	Interaction with Side A		
	Interaction with Side B		

You will have observed that, without the battery, the nail cannot pick up any paper clips. It is not a magnet. However, it does feel the magnetic force. Either end of the nail is attracted equally to either pole of the round magnet. You can play with two of the round magnets to confirm that a magnet has poles that behave differently. Depending on which sides are facing each other, you will observe attraction or repulsion.

The Table below highlights the important differences among non-magnetic materials, magnetic materials, and magnets:

Am I a Magnet ... or Just Magnetic Material ... or Not Magnetic At All?				
TYPE OF MATERIAL	FEELS ≈MAGNETIC FORCE	EXERTS MAGETIC FORCE	HAS TWO DIFFERENT POLES	ATTRACTS AND REPELS
NON-MAGNETIC MATERIAL	✗	✗	✗	✗
MAGNETIC MATERIAL	✓	✗	✗	✗
MAGNET	✓	✓	✓	✓

You should have observed that when the wrapped nail is connected to the battery, it attracts paper clips. Further, the two ends of the nail now behave differently from each other when they are tested with the round magnet. Without electricity flowing in the wire, the two ends are the same. When the battery is connected, the two ends behave differently. Flowing electricity changes the nail with the wire around it from a magnetic material into a magnet. If you are very patient and observant, you can also see some repelling between an end of the nail and a side of the round magnet.

Here's another experiment that you can do to explore electricity and magnetism. Carefully strip all the insulation off the 30 cm long piece of 20 gauge wire. Separate one of the thin copper strands, and remove it from the others. Test it with a stack of 5 round magnets to see if it is non-magnetic, magnetic, or a magnet. Write down your result.

Tape one end of the wire to the negative bottom of the D size battery, and tape the other end to the positive top of the battery. Now electricity is flowing through the wire. You can feel it getting warmer. Carefully test all around the wire with both sides of the stack of magnets. You should be able to confirm that the copper wire now feels the magnetic force, and it shows both attraction and repulsion. The flowing electricity has made the copper wire into a weak magnet. Make sure you disconnect the wire from the battery!

Electricity can be made by simply moving magnets past wires.

These two experiments show that electricity and magnetism are related to each other. Most of us never see inside the power plants where our electric currents are generated. If we did, we would not have to do experiments to learn that electricity and magnetism are closely related to each other. You would know it because the guided tour would emphasize that the power station generates electricity by forcing metal wires to move in an area that is surrounded by magnets. When wires move the right way in the presence of magnets, electricity flows through the wires. That flow of electrons can then be guided through other wires until it reaches the devices that we use.

You can do a very cool experiment to prove to yourself that electricity can be made by simply moving magnets past wires.[2] The illustration shows what the experiment looks like. A clear tube has five round magnets inside it. The middle of the tube has a lot of thin wire wrapped around it. The two ends of the wire are connected to an LED light. When the magnets move past the wire, this motion causes electricity to flow in the wires, and this electricity lights up the bulb. This is a "Look ma, no batteries" experiment.

[2] From "Stripped Down Generator," adapted with permission from the Exploratorium, from the book *Square Wheels and Other Easy-to-Build Hands-On Science Activities.* ©2002 Exploratorium, www.exploratorium.edu

You can try this experiment two different ways. The first is to hold this book in front of you, and move it side-to-side very fast so the illustration moves back and forth across your eyes. Say to yourself, "I am getting sleepy, and I am observing the light go on and off." Sometimes this works, but it is not very scientific.

The more scientific way involves doing the experiment. The directions are in the Chapter 5 section of the guidetoscience website. It is also in the *Dr. Art Does Science* DVD (see page ix).

The electromagnet, the strand of copper wire connected to the battery, the power plant guided tour, and the moving magnets in the tube experiment all show that electricity and magnetism are closely related. Flowing electricity can make a nail become a magnet, and turn a thin strand of wire into a magnet. We can make electricity flow by moving wires and magnets near each other. All these situations reveal a very deep feature of electricity and magnetism. They are both part of the same force, which scientists call electromagnetism.

BIG IDEA

Electricity and magnetism are both part of the same force, which scientists call electromagnetism.

Electromagnetism Is The Glue Of Matter

The structure of atoms and molecules depends on the electromagnetic force. Think about the atom with its positively charged central nucleus and its negatively charged electrons. The electromagnetic attraction between these opposite charges holds the atom together.

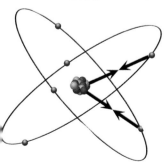

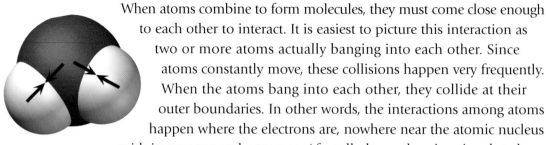

When atoms combine to form molecules, they must come close enough to each other to interact. It is easiest to picture this interaction as two or more atoms actually banging into each other. Since atoms constantly move, these collisions happen very frequently. When the atoms bang into each other, they collide at their outer boundaries. In other words, the interactions among atoms happen where the electrons are, nowhere near the atomic nucleus with its protons and neutrons. After all, the nucleus is a tiny dot, deep within the atom, occupying less than 0.001% of its volume.

Chemistry is the science that investigates how atoms bond with each other to form molecules. These bonds involve the sharing of electrons. Atoms connect with each other to form molecules by sharing electrons. In other words, the electromagnetic force holds atoms together in molecules.

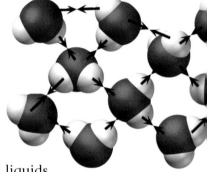

In Dr. Art's 50th Anniversary Ball, we modeled how molecules connect with each other in liquids and solids. These connections occur because positive parts of one molecule and negative parts of a different molecule attract each other. Solids and liquids exist because of electromagnetism, the glue of matter.

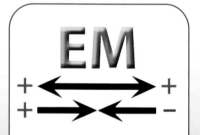

BIG IDEA

Electromagnitism is the glue of matter.

Forces Within The Atom

After Rutherford's positively charged subatomic bullets came bouncing back at him from the thin sheet of gold, scientist knew that the negative electrons are located in the outer boundaries of the atom, and that the positive protons are located in the atom's center. They also knew that the electromagnetic attraction is very strong between positively charged and negatively charged objects. Both of these facts meant they had a problem in really understanding the structure of the atom.

STOP & THINK: Why did scientists have a problem with the locations of the protons and the electrons?

How could the protons and electrons stay separated? The electromagnetic force should pull the electrons into the nucleus. Why do they remain at the atom's outer edges?

If I were a nice guy, I would never tell you about a problem where I could not really explain the answer to you. Unfortunately, that is what I just did.

Up until now, I have talked about the space between the protons and the electrons as being empty space. If that space were truly empty, then the electromagnetic attraction would do just what we expect—it would pull the electrons into the nucleus.

It turns out that the space inside the atom is a very weird space. In fact, the atom is so weird that scientists in the early 1900s had to invent a whole new field of science, called quantum mechanics, to figure it out. I will not even try to explain quantum mechanics in this book. I once embarrassed myself even more than usual by trying to play the advanced levels of a computer game even though I barely knew how to move on the screen or select any options. In this book, we are learning the basics of the science game. Quantum mechanics is for very advanced players.

I can tell you that this advanced science teaches that electrons strongly resist being pushed closer to the nucleus. They feel the electromagnetic attraction of the positively charged nucleus, but they cannot go there. Quantum mechanics explains why the electrons remain at the outer edges of the atom.

In trying to figure out the structure of the atom, scientists faced another electromagnetic puzzle. Positive charges repel each other. The nucleus is packed with positively charged protons. For example, the nucleus of a gold atom has 79 protons packed into its tiny nucleus. These positive charges are right next to each other, so the electromagnetism pushing them apart must be very strong. What holds the atomic nucleus together?

It turns out that there is another force in nature called the strong nuclear force. For two protons in an atomic nucleus, this force is about 20 times stronger than the electromagnetic force. That is why the strong nuclear force can hold the positively charged protons together even though electromagnetism would make them fly apart. As we shall explore in the next chapter, the strong nuclear force powers the Sun and other stars. It is also the force that our society uses in nuclear power plants and in atomic bombs.

Matter, Energy, Forces

Let's step back and consider how far we have come in understanding our world. We are systems made of many kinds of molecules. Any piece of matter that we observe, no matter how tiny, consists of gazillions of molecules. We do not experience the properties of individual molecules. We experience the properties of systems of molecules. These properties include hardness, color, texture, temperature, density, and shape.

The Sun, nuclear power plants, and hydrogen bombs all show the power of the strong nuclear force.

Molecules constantly move and jiggle. As a result, they have a tendency to move away from each other. The electromagnetic force holds the molecules together in solids and liquids.

In solids, the individual molecules connect relatively tightly so that the solid as a whole keeps its volume and its shape. In a liquid, the connections between molecules are weaker. As a result, a liquid can change its shape (flow), but it cannot change its volume. The molecules cannot get further away from each other, even if there is more room in the container. In gases, the molecules hardly interact with each other at all. A gas will adapt to the shape of its container, and it will fill whatever volume is available to it.

Molecules are made of atoms. Whenever two or more atoms combine with each other, they form a molecule. The electromagnetic force holds the atoms together in molecules. Atoms bond together to form molecules much more strongly than molecules connect with each other in solids or liquids. In Dr. Art's 50th Anniversary Ball, the DJ needed professional wrestlers to separate the husbands and wives from each other. In contrast, couples readily released the ribbons that connected them with other couples.

Solid ice cubes keep their shape. Liquid water adapts to the shape of the glass, and gas bubbles escape to join the outside air.

Atoms themselves are made of subatomic particles with different electrical charges (positively charged protons, negatively charged electrons, and uncharged neutrons). The electromagnetic force holds the protons and electrons together within the atom. Despite their strong attraction for each other, they remain separated, with the electrons located in the atom's outer boundaries. Quantum mechanics explains why the electrons remain at the outer edge of the atom.

The protons and neutrons are located in the atom's nucleus. The strong nuclear force keeps the protons bound together even though the electromagnetic force would make them fly apart.

Three Forces		
FORCE	STRENGTH	PROPERTIES
GRAVITY G	Weak. However, lots of mass in the same place adds up to a strong force.	Only attracts. Responsible for structure of solar system, galaxies, moons orbiting planets.
ELECTROMAGNETISM EM + + + −	Millions of times stronger than gravity.	Attracts and repels. Holds atom together, connects atoms, connects molecules.
STRONG NUCLEAR SN	20 or more times stronger than electromagnetism.	Only attracts. Responsible for structure of atomic nucleus.

Back at our everyday level of reality, we experience changes in matter that are related to energy. We note that energy readily changes from one form to another. Forms of energy that we experience include heat, light, motion, electric current, and chemical energy. The Law of Energy Conservation tells us that whenever anything happens, the total amount of energy remains constant.

When we experience or observe forces, both matter and energy are involved. At our level of reality, we have some limited direct experience of electricity and magnetism. To us, they usually appear to be very different from each other. Yet, they are actually both the same thing— electromagnetism. The features of electricity and magnetism that we observe at our level of reality are the tip of the electromagnetic iceberg. The electricity and magnetism that we experience provide clues that all matter has electrical and magnetic properties. So far, humans have learned to take advantage of just a small proportion of the electromagnetic properties of matter.

The features of electricity and magnetism that we observe are the tip of the electromagnetic iceberg.

BIG IDEA

Force Fields

You may remember that Newton never understood how gravity worked. He proved that it exists, and that it works exactly the same way throughout the solar system as it does on Earth. We still use his math equations for gravity to guide our rockets when we send them to other planets and moons. Newton could do all that without really understanding "action at a distance," how one object can influence another object without actually touching it.

Electromagnetism has that same puzzling property. One reason that magnets fascinate us is that we can actually feel the force of repulsion or attraction in the empty space between two magnets. Static electricity also fascinates us because we can see the piece of paper jumping off the table or the spark jumping from our finger to the doorknob. Just like gravity, electromagnetism enables objects to make other objects move without actually touching them.

Today scientists use the term "field" to explain this action at a distance. Magnets provide the easiest way to see a force field. You can buy iron filings, very small pieces of iron, and use them to visualize magnetic fields. The illustration shows the way that iron filings become arranged when they are exposed to a magnet. Each little iron filing shows us the shape of the electromagnetic field in its location. All together, they help us visualize what scientists call the electromagnetic field of the magnet.

With iron filings, we can see that the field gets weaker as the distance from the object increases. With very sensitive devices, scientists can actually measure gravitational and electromagnetic fields thousands of miles away from an object that is the source of the field. In fact, the fields never end. They just keep getting weaker and weaker to the point where even our most sensitive devices cannot measure them.

Saturn, 1.4 billion kilometers away from the Sun, is held in its orbit by the Sun's gravitational field. Its distance from the Sun is about ten times Earth's distance from the Sun.

This idea of fields changes the way we visualize our world. There is no such thing as empty space. On Earth, invisible air is filled with molecules, gravitational fields, and electromagnetic fields. Even in outer space, where there are essentially no molecules, space is still filled with these fields.

Each of us and anything that we can sense is a source of gravitational and electromagnetic fields. Each of us and anything we can sense is influenced by the gravitational and electromagnetic fields of everything around us. There are no isolated things or empty space. Everything is connected to everything else.

Earlier in this book we encountered the Awesome Systems Idea. Now we have the **Awesome Connections Idea**.

Dr. Art is very happy to report that this is a systems view of the world. Systems are about things that connect with and influence each other. Systems are never about an isolated thing that has no connections. Everything that exists is connected in mind-boggling ways with everything else that exists.

Awesome Idea

CONNECTIONS
Everything is connected to and affects everything else.

STOP & THINK

Scientists often make models to try to understand the things they are investigating. For example, after shooting subatomic bullets at a thin sheet of gold, Rutherford developed a model of the atom featuring a very small, positively charged nucleus. To help you visualize the structure of the atom, I used the model of a marble in the middle of the Louisiana Superdome with electrons as wisps of dust on the building's outer edges (page 40).

Most of us use models in our recreation and work. We interact with computer and other games as if they are real things. We watch movies filled with models of reality. We like it when the game or movie tricks us into thinking that it is real.

Scientists use models because it helps them become clearer in their own thinking and in communicating their ideas to others. The models can take many forms. A model can even be as weird as using an Anniversary Ball to explain the differences between solids, liquids, and gases.

In addition to diving into their models like we do with games and movies, scientists also step back from their models to analyze them. They try to figure out how the model is different from the reality, and whether those differences cause them to make mistakes in their thinking. They wonder how they can change their models to make them represent reality more accurately.

This chapter includes a simple model of how a power station makes electricity. By moving magnets back and forth in a tube that has lots of wrapped electric wire, we cause electricity to flow in the wire (page 74). This is a good model because the same properties of electromagnetism cause electricity to flow in power stations. Since this model does not burn fuel, it is not a good model if we want to try to understand how power stations can cause air pollution.

As you read this book, be aware of the models that I use. Ask yourself if they help you understand the ideas. See if you can make up your own models to explain the ideas to yourself and others. The next chapter has lots of models, so you can start practicing right away.

PUTTING THE YOU IN UNIVERSE

The U Word

Our universe is all the matter and energy that shares this same space and time. As we keep learning more about the universe, we discover that it is far more amazing than we can imagine.

We once considered Earth to be the center of the universe. Now we know that the Sun is just one star among billions in a collection of stars that we call the Milky Way galaxy. The photo on the bottom of the next page shows a galaxy that is similar in shape to ours. Our solar system is located in one of the spiral "arms," about two-thirds of the way from the center to the edge of the beautiful Milky Way galaxy.

Some people have the mistaken notion when they see the Milky Way in the sky, that they are somehow looking at the Milky Way from a position outside of the galaxy. The ragged, hazy band of light circling the night sky that we call the Milky Way is actually how the center of the galaxy appears as we look at it from our location within one of the galaxy's spiral arms.

People who live in cities rarely see how many stars there are in the sky. The city lights make it hard for us to see them. On clear nights in dark areas, the sky appears filled with thousands of stars, and a band of hazy light also circles the night sky. People in all cultures have noted this special band of light. When we see it, we say, "Hey! Look at the Milky Way!"

Well, it turns out that whenever we see stars in the sky, we are already looking at the Milky Way. All the thousands of stars that we see in the sky are part of the Milky Way galaxy. When we look toward the center of the galaxy, we see that distant center as a hazy band of light. It looks so special that we call it the Milky Way. It is actually the center of the Milky Way, not the whole thing.

This is what the Milky Way would look like if we could see it from a position outside the galaxy.

As recently as the early 1900s, scientists thought that our galaxy was the entire universe. Now we know that the universe has billions of galaxies, each one with its own collection of huge numbers of stars.

How Long Is A Light Year?

The very closest galaxy, called Andromeda, is 20 times as far away from us as the width of the Milky Way galaxy. Andromeda is so far away from us that we need a new way of describing that distance. Instead of using kilometers or miles, scientists describe the distance from here to Andromeda as being 2,000,000 light years.

If we could somehow leave the Milky Way, we would have to travel 2,000,000 light years before we reached Andromeda. In other words, even if we could somehow travel at the speed of light, the trip would last two million years. For 95% of our journey, we would be in empty space, with scarcely any molecules around us. That would definitely be a very long, strange trip.

A light year is the distance that light, speeding at the rate of 300,000 kilometers per second, will travel in one year. To calculate how far light travels in one year, we need to multiply its speed in kilometers per second times the number of seconds in a year.

$$300,000 \frac{km}{second} \times 60 \frac{seconds}{minute} \times 60 \frac{minutes}{hour} \times 24 \frac{hours}{day} \times 365 \frac{days}{year} = 9,500,000,000 \frac{km}{year}$$

So light travels 9,500,000,000 kilometers in one year. In ten years, light travels ten times that distance, which would be 10 light years.

Some people get confused because the term light year has the word "year," a word that we usually use for time, not for distance. You could get used to this idea by describing other distances in terms of biking minutes or car hours. Perhaps your favorite movie theater is 40 biking minutes away, or 20 bus minutes away when the traffic is good. A refrigerator with a tasty treat could be just 7 running seconds away from your bedroom. For an infant, it could be 25 crawling seconds away.

Just 25 crawling seconds away.

Just 20 subway minutes away.

Imagine that you have an eccentric, rich aunt named Mathematica. She lives 300 kilometers away, and she always brings fantastic presents. Aunt Mathematica loves science and math. Since she knows that you are reading Chapter 6 of *Dr. Art's Guide to Science*, she says she will visit after you write her and tell her how far away she lives in terms of bicycle hours, running days, and light seconds. She says that she can bike 20 km per hour, run 15 km in a day, and that light travels at 300,000 km per second. What will you write her?

Dear Aunt Mathematica,

I am looking forward to your visit. I hope you can get here real soon. The distance here from your home is 15 bicycle hours. If you are running, it is still the same distance, but it is going to feel longer because it is 20 running days. Maybe you should hop on a ray of light because it is less than one light second away.

Don't forget, the last time you visited you promised to tell me the secret of how you got your name.

Levels Of Reality

We are exploring the universe from the subatomic to the cosmic levels. At the smallest sizes, subatomic particles join to form atoms. These atoms combine with each other to form molecules such as water, carbon dioxide, and proteins. Gazillions of molecules link with each other to form the level of reality in which we normally operate. Our planet is part of a solar system located in the immense Milky Way galaxy. Our universe contains billions of galaxies.

These levels involve extremely small numbers (such as 0.0000001 cm for the size of atoms) and unimaginably large numbers (like the distance of a light year). Scientists and mathematicians get tired of writing and having to count zeros. They use the "powers of ten" method to write really small and really big numbers.

In this method, a thousand (1,000) is written as 10^3. One million (1,000,000) is written as 10^6 (pronounced ten to the sixth power, or just ten to the six). Simply count the digits after the one, and you have the power number.

For really small numbers, one thousandth (0.001) is written as 10^{-3}. One millionth is written as 10^{-6} (pronounced ten to the minus six). Simply count the digits to the right of the decimal point, and you have the negative power number.

GALAXY
Billions of stars
connected by gravity

SOLAR SYSTEM
9 planets and othe[r]
bodies orbit the Su[n]

UNIVERSE
Billions of galaxies

Milky Way: 10^{21}

Now I can share with you the famous **Powers of Ten** description of the levels of our universe, first popularized by two husband-wife teams (scientists Philip and Phylis Morrison, and artists Charles and Ray Eames). We start with our level of reality, and the photo of a bee on a flower.

From ground level we jump to bigger and bigger sizes. The flower is located in San Francisco's Golden Gate Park. Jumping five powers of ten, we have a view of the San Francisco Bay Area from 100 km above the ground. Now we have to jump another two powers of ten to get a great view of our entire planet. From there we have to jump two more powers of ten to see Moon's orbit around Earth. Another four powers of ten enable us to see all the planets orbiting the Sun. From the solar system, we have to leap eight more powers of ten to get a great view of the Milky Way galaxy.

Solar System:
10^{13}

**Moon orbit of
Earth: 10^9**

Earth: 10^7

Satellite image of
San Francisco Bay
Area: 10^5

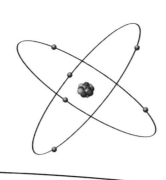

OUR LEVEL
anet with millions of
ferent kinds of things

ATOMIC
92 different kinds of atoms
make up the elements

SUBATOMIC
3 particles that
"make up" the atom

Returning to our ground level of the bee on the flower, we can magnify one hundred times so we can see beautiful details of the bee's head. Magnifying another four powers of ten, we can see a red blood cell in the bee's blood. Exploring deeper another three powers of ten smaller (to the size of 10^{-9} meters), we are just beginning to be able to make images of atoms connected to each other. We have no photographic images of smaller structures, but scientists have explored the nature of reality at levels of 10^{-20} meters, and even smaller.

Stars Are Born

You may have heard or read that our universe began with a "Big Bang." Before the Big Bang theory, scientists thought that the universe has always existed with more or less the same types of matter. However, they kept finding more and more evidence that our universe began about fifteen billion years ago, and that it has gone through amazing changes since its beginning.

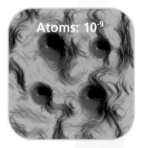
Atoms: 10^{-9}

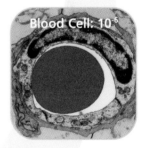
Blood Cell: 10^{-6}

Bee Head: 10^{-2}

We are somewhere in the middle of an awesome reality that expands many powers of ten above us and submerges many powers of ten below us.

BIG IDEA

It now seems fairly certain that early in its history, the universe did not contain any stars or galaxies. In its infancy, our universe had only hydrogen and helium, the two simplest elements (hydrogen has one proton; helium has two protons). These atoms were spread evenly throughout the early universe, with about 75% hydrogen and 25% helium.

What saved our universe from becoming a boring, dark place consisting only of hydrogen and helium gas spread out in space? Gravity created exciting new possibilities for our universe. Slowly, over time, gravity began to cause the hydrogen and helium to gather in huge clumps with empty spaces in between.

Since the force of gravity increases with the amount of matter, the more stuff that gathers in one location, the more it attracts any other stuff to the vicinity. As a result, gas clouds containing hydrogen and helium formed and grew.

Before this clumping happened, every place in the early universe looked almost exactly like every other place. After gravity started to cause the hydrogen and helium gas to clump, our universe became more interesting. Some parts of the universe featured large, concentrated clouds of hydrogen and helium. The areas in between became emptier, containing fewer and fewer atoms.

Over time, the universe became more interesting.

About 100 million years after the Big Bang, the gas clouds had gathered so much gas that a completely new thing happened. Some of these clouds had gathered 100 or more times as much mass as currently exists in our Sun. What happens when gravity causes so many atoms to accumulate in one location? The atoms that are close to the center experience enormous pressure from the mass of all the outer atoms pressing in on them. That pressure drastically changes the shape and behavior of the center atoms.

An atom consists of a tiny nucleus containing almost all the mass (protons and neutrons) surrounded by distant electrons. The pressure of all the outer atoms pressing in towards the center causes the interior gas atoms to smash into each other, and breaks their electronic shells. As a result, protons and neutrons from different atoms are crushed together by the immense gravitational pressure, and they combine to form new, bigger atomic nuclei (plural of nucleus).

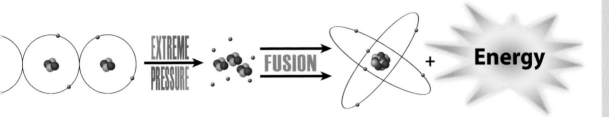

The process that I just described is called nuclear fusion. This process causes huge amounts of energy to be released. The gas clouds glowed and then shined brightly. Stars had been born. Their starlight illuminated that our universe had become a very interesting place with great new possibilities.

Energymatter

Wait a second, wait a second! What happened to the Law of Conservation of Energy? Where did all this energy come from?

We have to go to the last century's most famous scientist for the answer. Albert Einstein taught us that matter and energy are actually two forms of the same thing. I like to call it energymatter.

Remember when you used to think that electricity and magnetism are completely different from each other? Then you realized that they are both part of a bigger thing called electromagnetism. Einstein taught us that the basic stuff of the universe is energymatter. What we call energy and what we call matter are really two different ways of experiencing energymatter. Matter can change into energy, and energy can morph into matter.

$$E=mc^2$$

At our level of everyday reality, we experience energymatter as either energy or as matter. We experience them as being very different. Physicists and engineers have working knowledge of energymatter. They experience matter and energy changing into each other in nuclear power plants, in very specialized physics experiments, and in their observations of stars and galaxies.

Not only are energy and matter part of the same thing, an equation tells us how they are related to each other. Einstein's famous equation $E = mc^2$ exactly quantifies the relationship between matter and energy. When matter changes into energy, the amount of energy (E) released is equal to the mass (m, amount of matter) that is changing times the speed of light squared (c^2). Since the speed of light squared is a very big number, we get a lot of energy (E) from a little bit of matter. For example, our Sun releases heat and light because of nuclear fusion. The Sun converts 5 million tons of nuclear mass into energy every second. Fortunately, it has enough matter so it can keep doing this for another five billion years.

Not only does matter change into energy, but energy changes into matter. Subatomic particles can pop into existence from energy and then disappear back into energy. This would be a great party trick if it happened at our level of reality.

Did you know?

If all the mass of this page were converted to energy, the energy released would destroy a small city.

What happened to the Law of Energy Conservation? It has become an even bigger idea. We can now call it the Conservation of Energymatter. Whenever anything happens in the universe, the amount of energymatter at the start is exactly equal to the amount of energymatter at the end. Energymatter is never created or destroyed. The earlier Law of Energy Conservation is still true as long as matter is not changing into energy, or energy is not changing into matter. Energymatter is so important and mind-boggling that I call it the Awesome Energymatter Idea.

Where Everything Else Came From

Some of you may have noticed that the only elements after the Big Bang were hydrogen and helium. These two gases are wonderful, but they cannot form Earth-like planets or living organisms. Yet, here we exist on planet Earth. Since we and Earth consist of atoms that are much bigger and more complicated than hydrogen and helium, some process must have formed these bigger atoms. Where did the larger elements come from?

Awesome Idea

ENERGYMATTER
Our universe consists of energymatter. Energy and matter are part of the same thing, converting into each other according to $E = mc^2$.

To understand the origin of the larger elements, we need to explore what happens in stars. By Earth standards, stars contain enormous amounts of matter. Our Sun is a very average star, and it contains 300,000 times as much mass as our planet. Many stars are much larger than our Sun.

As I described earlier in this chapter, the pressure of all the mass pushing in causes dramatic changes in the atoms that are close to the center of a star. Most of the star's mass is hydrogen, and the hydrogen nucleus has one proton. The outer electronic shells shatter and the nuclei get forced closer and closer together. Through nuclear fusion, hydrogen nuclei combine to form helium, which has two protons in its nucleus. As this happens, some of the mass changes into a huge amount of energy that then explodes outward from the center.

Stars exist in a delicately balanced condition. The mass of all the atoms tends to force the star sphere to become denser and smaller. This same pressure causes the interior hydrogen atoms to combine with each other. In this nuclear fusion process, tremendous amounts of energy are released. This energy pushes the gas atoms outward. Therefore, stars constantly experience forces that tend to make them implode (drastically shrink in size) and explode. All stars balance the forces that are pulling inward (gravity) and pushing outward (nuclear explosions).

Astronomers often describe stars as having life cycles. A star is born when enough hydrogen atoms have gathered together to create the pressure that starts the nuclear fusion process. A star enters the main part of its "life" when a balance is established between the forces pulling in and pushing out. A star the size of our Sun can fuse its hydrogen more or less constantly for ten billion years or longer.

After stars have consumed their hydrogen fuel, they enter old age. These older stars begin using their helium as nuclear fuel. Helium nuclei combine with protons or with other helium nuclei to form larger elements. This common star process explains how our universe can contain bigger atoms than hydrogen and helium. For example, three helium nuclei combine to form carbon with its six protons. All of Earth's living beings are carbon-based organisms. That carbon was made in stars by this nuclear fusion process.

If we can describe stars as being born, living, and getting old, is there any sense in which we can describe stars as dying? Actually, the death of stars provides one of the keys to understanding our universe. Some stars bigger than our Sun end their lives in extremely violent explosions. These large stars can explode in a way that releases more energy in a few weeks than our Sun releases during all of its ten billion years. Astronomers call this explosion a **supernova**. An average galaxy will have three supernova events every century.

BIG IDEA

Nuclear fusion in stars makes all the elements except hydrogen.

These supernova events generate such intense heat and pressures that atoms fuse together to create all the elements except hydrogen. We are used to thinking of explosions as causing things to break apart. Nuclear fusion explosions are very different—the atoms combine to form bigger atoms. The huge energy of the explosion arises because some of the mass changes into energy. Supernova explosions are important because they help generate all the heavier elements, and because they spread all the elements into the galaxy.

This stardust spreads within a galaxy and mixes with the existing clouds of hydrogen, helium, and other elements. The shockwaves from supernova explosions can also push the gas close enough together that they form a star. Some of the stardust can end up as planets that orbit the new star. Thus, not only can stars die, they can also be reborn as new stars and as planets.

Birth Of Our Solar System

Approximately 4,500,000,000 years ago, a large cloud of gas started to rapidly contract in our small neighborhood of the Milky Way galaxy. A shockwave from a relatively nearby supernova probably triggered this event. This gas cloud contained significant amounts of heavier elements in addition to the universal hydrogen and helium. The triggering supernova injected its heavier elements into the gas cloud. Our Sun and all the bodies of the solar system (planets, moons, asteroids) formed from this same mixture of hydrogen, helium, and heavier elements.

The vast majority of the matter condensed in the center, ignited nuclear fusion of the hydrogen gas, and became our Sun. The rest of the gas and dust orbited the Sun, and eventually formed the planets, moons, asteroids, and comets.

Compared with other stars in the Milky Way, the Sun appears to be an average star. From our local point of view, the Sun is the star of our solar system. For us, it is a very special star in that is located only 93,000,000 miles away, rather than light years in the distance. It has 740 times more mass than all the planets combined. We could fit one million Earths inside the Sun.

BIG IDEA

Earth is essentially stardust.

Our Sun consists of 70% hydrogen, 28% helium, and 2% heavier elements. All the Sun's hydrogen and most of its helium came into existence in the first few minutes of the universe. The rest of the helium and all of the Sun's heavier elements were made in stars millions of years after the Big Bang.

Earth is essentially stardust. Consider an oxygen atom that you are breathing here on Earth at this very moment. Each oxygen atom has eight protons. These protons first appeared as hydrogen and helium atoms in the beginning of our universe. They gathered with other hydrogen and helium atoms to become a star in the Milky Way galaxy. In that star's nuclear fusion processes, these very simple atoms combined to form the larger oxygen atom with its eight protons.

When the star exploded, the oxygen atom mixed with the other gases in the Milky Way. It was then attracted to a swirling collection of hydrogen, helium, and other heavier elements that formed our solar system. Most of the stuff became the Sun, but a small percentage formed the planets orbiting the Sun. The oxygen atom combined with carbon, and became part of an Earth rock.

A calcium atom in your front tooth—made in a star more than 4.5 billion years ago.

Like everything on Earth, we consist of atoms that were made in stars billions of years ago.

A nitrogen atom in one of your heart cells—made in a star more than 4.5 billion years ago.

An oxygen atom in a water molecule in your blood—made in a star more than 4.5 billion years ago.

A carbon atom that has been flowing in and out of living organisms since the beginning of life on this planet—made in a star more than 4.5 billion years ago.

A sodium atom in a nerve in your toe—made in a star more than 4.5 billion years ago.

Scale Models

At the end of the last chapter, I wrote that scientists use models to describe the things they investigate. Models come in different sizes. Dinosaur models in a museum are usually as large as the original dinosaur. In contrast, the museum store might have toy dinosaur models that fit in a child's hand. Both models represent the same thing, but they differ in scale.

If a model is the same size as the original, we say that the scale is 1 to 1. If the model is one tenth the size of the original, we say that the scale is 1 to 10. Let's say we make a dinosaur model that is one tenth the size of the original. If the dinosaur's head is 2 meters long, the head in our model would be 0.2 meters long.

The girl and dinosaur skull were life-size (1 to 1 scale) in the museum. What do you think the scale is in this photo?

Scale models can be very helpful for very large systems, such as the solar system or the Milky Way galaxy. We will start with planet Earth, and use the "Cosmic Sizes and Distances" Table below as our guide.

Previous chapters have used Tables as a way to summarize lots of information. This Table is packed with food for our minds, so we are going to spend some time figuring out what it all means.

If Earth is a marble and the Moon is a bead, would the Moon be located at point A, B, or C?

Reading across the Earth row, the Cosmic Sizes and Distances Table shows that our planet has a diameter of 12,742 kilometers (km). Each kilometer is about 5/8 of a mile, so Earth's diameter is about

Cosmic Sizes and Distances

OBJECT	REAL DIAMETER	SCALED DIAMETER	REAL DISTANCE FROM EARTH	SCALED DISTANCE FROM EARTH
EARTH	12,742 km	Small marble 1 cm	Starting location	Starting location
MOON	3,476 km	Plastic bead	380,000 km	30 cm 0.3 meters 1 foot
SUN	1,400,000 km 100 times that of Earth	Large beach ball	150,000,000 km	120 meters about length of football or soccer field
NEAREST STAR	Similar to the Sun	Large beach ball	Five light years 48 million million km	40,000 km
MILKY WAY	100,000 light years	About five times the real distance to the Sun	Distant edge is about 75,000 light years away	15,000 times further away than nearest star
ANDROMEDA GALAXY	160,000 light years	About eight times the real distance to the Sun	2,000,000 light years away	20 times further than the edge of Milky Way

A light year is the distance that light travels in one year.   1 light year = 9,500,000,000,000 km = 6,000,000,000,000 miles.

8,000 miles. The "Scaled Diameter" column tells us that we are going to use a marble about 1 centimeter (cm) wide to represent planet Earth.

Looking at the Moon row, we see that it is about one quarter the diameter of Earth. It could be represented by something a quarter the size of the marble, such as a small plastic bead. How far from the marble (Earth) should we put the bead (Moon)? The Table tells us that the real distance from Earth to the Moon is 380,000 km.

To be accurate, we want to use the same scale to represent the distance between the objects as we use for the sizes of the objects themselves. We continue to use a small marble (top left of page 100) to represent planet Earth. Which location (A, B, or C) most accurately represents the distance of the Moon (plastic bead) from Earth?

We used a marble with a diameter of 1 cm to represent the 12,742 km diameter of planet Earth. Therefore, our scale is:

C

1 cm = 12,742 km, or we can write it as

1 cm/12,742 km (one cm per 12,742 km).

Since the Moon is 380,000 km away, we can calculate:

380,000 km times 1cm/12,742 km = 30 cm

(note that the km in the numerator and denominator cancel each other, so our answer is in cm).

In other words, if the Earth is 1 cm wide, then the Moon should be 0.25 cm wide, and it should be placed 30 cm (1 foot) away from the marble. So, the bead at location C correctly represents both the size of the Moon and its distance relative to Earth.

Here's a great way to entertain your friends. Show them a marble and a bead. Tell them what each one represents, and ask them how far apart the marble and bead should be. After a while, you can also ask them, "How big an object should we use to represent the Sun, and how far away from the marble would it be?"

This photo shows an eclipse, where the Moon blocks our view of the Sun. Why do the Sun and Moon appear to be about the same size?

If you have the right kind of friends, they will run home to get their copies of *Dr. Art's Guide to Science*. They will then run back with the books open to page 100, and show you the Sun row from the Table, shouting excitedly, "See that beach ball 120 meters back there? That's the Sun shining on our little marble."

If you then look from your Earth marble toward the plastic bead about a third of meter away and the beach ball 120 meters away, the distant beach ball (the Sun) will look about the same size as the nearby plastic bead (the Moon). This result is similar to our normal experience that the Sun and Moon look about the same size in the sky.

The information in the Cosmic Sizes and Distances Table tells us that while the Sun is about 400 times wider than the Moon (1,400,000 divided by 3,476 = 403), it is also 400 times further away (150,000,000 divided by 380,000 = 395). That is why the Sun and Moon look about the same size in the sky.

What about the stars we see at night? The nearest star is so far away that we describe its distance in light years, rather than kilometers. The Cosmic Sizes and Distance Table tells us that the nearest star is five light years away. Light from that star takes five years to reach us, so we are seeing the star the way it looked five years ago. If that star exploded today, we would not see the explosion until five years from now.

If we continue to use the same scale from our Cosmic Table, how far away would be put a beach ball representing the nearest star? We better get a space ship because we need to put that beach ball 40,000 kilometers away, four times the diameter of the entire planet. In our model, the Sun is a soccer field length away, and the nearest star is four times as far away as Earth's diameter. Despite all our science fiction movies, the nearest star is so far away that we have no hope of traveling there any time soon.

Summary

We live within an awesome universe that expands many powers of ten above us and submerges many powers of ten below us. We experience energy and matter as being very different, yet they are two forms of the same thing, energymatter.

Three forces explain how the energymatter in our universe behaves. Gravity causes it to clump into huge structures such as galaxies, stars, and planets. Electromagnetism glues matter into the forms that are familiar to us—atoms, molecules, liquids, and solids. The strong nuclear force holds protons together, making it possible for more than 90 different elements to exist.

We are children of the universe. All the hydrogen atoms in our bodies (approximately 10% of our mass) came into existence in the birth of our universe about thirteen billion years ago. The rest of our atoms were formed in stars in very distant times and places.

Like us, Earth is also stardust. In the next three chapters, we will explore matter, energy, and life on our stardust home planet.

STOP & THINK

In this chapter, we used math in scale models, powers of ten, and Einstein's famous equation. Mathematics has been called the language of science. This is true because math is a language of the universe. When scientists investigate the world, they often discover that things are related to each other according to very specific mathematical rules.

Scientists describe an equation such as Einstein's $E = mc^2$ as being elegant or beautiful. This equation reveals a very deep truth about the universe, that energy and matter are two forms of the same thing. Equally mind-boggling, the relationship involves the speed of light. The amount of energy is exactly equal to the amount of mass times the speed of light squared. Just five mathematical symbols (E, =, m, c, 2) describe one of the most important features of our universe. Among many other things, that equation explains how stars can give off energy for billions of years.

Perhaps I cannot help you appreciate the beauty in math, but I may be able to help you use math. One thing that I learned in school has helped me in many different situations. It is a simple rule: pay attention to the units. Make sure that the units cancel each other out so you get the answer that you want.

This rule helps with many situations in science. Keeping track of the units can also help in many real life situations. For example, I want to buy a new car, and I expect to drive 15,000 miles per year for 10 years. The calculation below shows how much money I would save by driving a hybrid car that gets 50 miles per gallon instead of a vehicle that averages 25 miles per gallon. I am assuming that gas will cost an average of $4.00 per gallon over the next ten years.

Hybrid Car: (15,000 miles/year)(1 gal/50 miles)($4.00/gal)(10 years) = $12,000

Regular Car: (15,000 miles/year)(1 gal/25 miles)($4.00/gal)(10 years) = $24,000

Over the ten years, I will save $12,000.

www.guidetoscience.net

HOME SWEET HOME

Chapter 7 –
Home Sweet Home

Earth In The Solar System

We can write and talk about the universe, but we really cannot picture it. In contrast, we know that the Milky Way galaxy is a beautiful spiral galaxy, just like those that we can see using our telescopes. Still, the immense width of the Milky Way galaxy (100,000 light years) prevents us from physically exploring it or emotionally bonding with it.

Rover tracks on Mars.

Our attitudes change when we come down in size to the level of the solar system. Throughout history, humans have emotionally connected with the Sun and its planets.

Of course, the Sun is the star of the solar system. It is the center, around which everything else travels. The Sun has 99.8% of the mass of the entire solar system, and it provides almost all the energy experienced on Earth.

This huge heavenly body, a sphere of exploding gas a million times larger than Earth, controls our lives. Our day is simply the amount of time it takes for Earth to spin a complete revolution on its axis. We experience daylight and night because we alternate between facing toward and away from the Sun. Our year is the amount of time it takes for Earth to complete its orbit around the Sun. Earth is a solar planet.

Earth Is Whole

Our planet is the third pebble out from the Sun, located between the

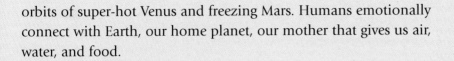

orbits of super-hot Venus and freezing Mars. Humans emotionally connect with Earth, our home planet, our mother that gives us air, water, and food.

One of humanity's major discoveries is that we live on a round planet. We laugh about the idea that Earth is flat. Yet, we ourselves are in the middle of an even greater change in the way that we should understand our planet. And most of us don't know about it.

When we realized that Earth is round, we learned how the places on our planet are physically connected to each other. We discovered that if we kept traveling in one direction, we would not fall off the edge. Instead we could go in a circle and return to our starting place. That was an important discovery for our ancestors.

Now we are learning something much more important than how the places on our planet are physically connected. We are discovering how Earth works as a whole system. Earth is not flat. Earth is much more than round. Earth is whole.

"Earth is Whole" means that all the planet's physical features and living organisms are interconnected. They work together in important and meaningful ways. The clouds, oceans, mountains, volcanoes, plants, bacteria, and animals all play important roles in determining how our planet works.

Scientists have established a new field of science called Earth systems science to study and discover how all these

BIG IDEA

"Earth is Whole" means that all the planet's physical features and living organisms are interconnected.

parts work together. I am sure you noticed the SYSTEMS word. Earth systems science combines the tools and ideas from many scientific disciplines including geology, biology, chemistry, physics, and computer science. Scientists use modern technologies to measure key features of our planet, such as the amount of gases in the atmosphere, and the temperature of the ocean in many locations. Satellites orbiting our planet provide enormous amounts of data that Earth systems scientists use to try to understand how our planet works, and the changes that are happening.

Of course, human beings do more than study and measure planet Earth. Just like any other organism, we are a part of this whole Earth system. More importantly, we now have a very challenging new role to play. For the first time in our history, we can dramatically change the way the planet works as a whole. There are so many of us and we have such powerful technologies that we can change Earth's climate, destroy its ozone shield, and dramatically alter the number and kinds of other organisms that share the planet with us.

BIG IDEA

Three parts of the Earth System:
- Earth's matter
- Earth's energy
- Earth's life

Can all of us live well on our planet without damaging the whole Earth system? To answer that question, we need to understand how our planet works. That sounds much more complicated than discovering that Earth is round. Fortunately, Earth systems science helps us understand the most important features of how our planet works.

We begin with the first systems question. What are the parts of the Earth system? I usually describe the Earth system in terms of the following three parts:

- **Earth's matter**
  - **Earth's energy**
    - **Earth's life**

In examining Earth as a whole, we are going to focus on Earth's matter (this Chapter), Earth's energy (Chapter 8) and Earth's life (Chapter 9).

In other words, we are going to examine the stuff (matter) that exists on Earth, the energy that makes things happen on Earth, and the organisms that make our planet unique in the solar system.

Earth's Solid Stuff

We can think of Earth's matter as a system that is made of three kinds of parts—solid stuff, liquid stuff, and gas stuff. Scientists don't like to use words like stuff; they call these parts of the Earth matter system its geosphere (solid), hydrosphere (water), and atmosphere (gas). We begin with the geosphere, Earth's solid stuff.

We can hardly imagine the conditions 4,500,000,000 (four billion five hundred million) years ago when Earth grew as a result of material constantly smashing into the growing planet. This young growing Earth was an exploding ball of melted rock/metal. As it eventually stabilized in size and cooled, the densest material settled to the center forming a metallic core that causes Earth's magnetic field.

We live on a thin crust of the less dense material. This crust remained floating on the top and solidified as it cooled. If we represent our planet as a globe that is four feet in diameter, the crust would occupy just the top one-quarter inch.

Most of the geosphere is very different than the solid Earth that we experience every day. Below us lies an almost completely unexplored world of denser rock and metal. This material, existing in conditions of very high temperatures and pressures, melts and flows, descending thousands of miles below our feet, homes, oceans, and forests. Earthquakes, volcanoes, and geysers indicate the high temperatures and pressures that exist in Earth's pressure cooker interior.

BIG IDEA

Earthquakes, volcanoes, and geysers indicate the high temperatures and pressures that exist in Earth's pressure cooker interior.

Scientists thought that today's continents and oceans had been the same for billions of years. In the 1960s, they found convincing evidence that changed this view of the Earth. Their measurements, data analysis, and theories caused a revolution in the Earth sciences.

This revolution taught us that Earth's surface consists of about a dozen huge plates that move into, away from, over, under, and next to each other. These plates float on top of a moving layer of hotter, more fluid material. The oceans and continents are contained as parts of these plates and move with them. So, instead of staying the same for billions of years, the continents and oceans keep changing their size and location.

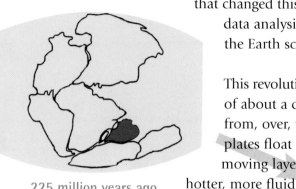

225 million years ago

135 million years ago

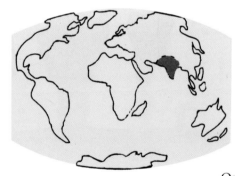

Today

Look how quickly they change! Only last month (okay, 225 million years ago—but that is last month on the geologic time scale), all the land mass was joined together as one huge supercontinent. By the time of the Jurassic Age (135 million years ago), some separation had occurred, but Africa was still practically joined to South America. Only in the last 135 million years (less than 5% of Earth's existence) has the mighty Atlantic Ocean formed between the Americas and Africa/Europe.

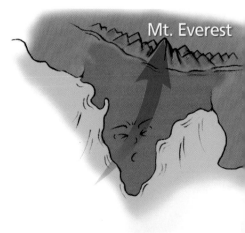

Mt. Everest

India (shown in red) provides another dramatic example of these changes. The current Indian landmass once existed well below the Equator, near the current location of Australia. During these hundreds of millions of years, the plate carrying today's India moved about 4,000 miles northward. As a result, India crashed into Asia approximately 40 million years ago and joined that continent. The combined surface crust of India and Asia crumpled upwards forming the Himalayas, the highest mountain range in the world, including all ten of the world's highest peaks.

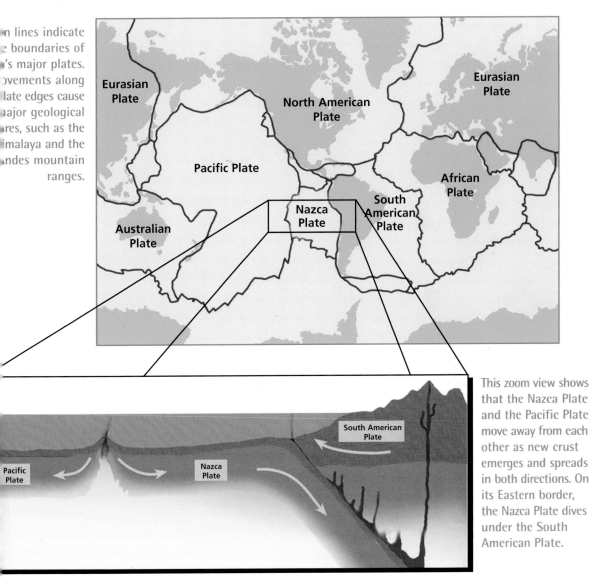

Thin lines indicate the boundaries of Earth's major plates. Movements along these plate edges cause major geological features, such as the Himalaya and the Andes mountain ranges.

This zoom view shows that the Nazca Plate and the Pacific Plate move away from each other as new crust emerges and spreads in both directions. On its Eastern border, the Nazca Plate dives under the South American Plate.

For our purposes in understanding planet Earth, we need to realize that these plates and their movements explain much more than continents coming together and being pulled apart. The movements of the plates are an important part of what you may have learned as the rock cycle.

Rocks on Earth's surface continually break down due to the forces of flowing water, chemical reactions, blowing wind, and crushing ice. This broken rock is eventually washed as sediment into the ocean. The net effect of this erosion is to lower the surface of the continents to sea level. From the point of view of geological time, this breaking down of Earth's mountains and surface is fairly rapid. In the course of just 18 million years, the continents would be reduced to sea level, and the oceans would cover the planet.

Why do we still have continents and mountains that reach miles into the air? Since the continents have existed for hundreds of millions of years, this erosion process must be balanced by a process that builds mountains. The movements of the plates explain many details of this mountain building.

Sometimes the mountains arise when continental masses collide as in the case of the Himalayas. Volcanoes demonstrate that mountains are also built from molten material in the Earth's interior. Eruption of lava does not happen just on land.

BIG IDEA

Earth has dry land because the processes that build mountains balance the processes that break them down.

The middle of the oceans is one of the most geologically active regions on our planet. It is a place where melted rock constantly flows from the interior to become new crust.

Earth's surface crust is constantly washed into the oceans. In places where one plate dives under another plate, this broken rock get sucked deep into Earth's interior where it melts. Eventually this melted rock emerges as lava to form new land rocks and new ocean floor.

The same rock material keeps getting used over and over again. When we explore the system of matter on planet Earth, the rock cycle is one reason that people often find themselves muttering, "matter cycles, matter cycles, matter cycles."

Rock Cycle

Earth's Liquid Stuff

Water blesses our planet and makes it appear beautifully blue from space. The presence of liquid water clearly distinguishes Earth from all the planets and moons of the solar system. In fact, water covers almost three times as much of Earth's surface as land does.

Water plays such an important role in our planet that Earth systems scientists extensively study the hydrosphere, the system of all Earth's water. This hydrosphere itself can be studied in terms of its parts—the oceans, frozen water in glaciers and polar ice caps, groundwater, surface fresh water, and water vapor in the atmosphere.

The parts of Earth's water system can also be identified as "water reservoirs," places where water occurs. (Scientists use the term reservoir to describe the different places where any substance, not just water, occurs.) The reservoir that holds the most water, 97.25% of all water on Earth, is the ocean. Check the Water Reservoir table to compare the amounts in other reservoirs, such as glaciers, groundwater, atmosphere, and living organisms.

We can also compare the different reservoirs by representing all of Earth's water as 1,000 milliliters (1 liter) in a

DID YOU KNOW?

Water covers almost three times as much of Earth's surface as land does.

Earth's Water Reservoirs

RESERVOIR	% OF TOTAL WATER	VOLUME IN CUBIC KILOMETERS (KM³)
Ocean	97.25%	1,370,000,000
Ice Caps & Glaciers	2.05%	29,000,000
Groundwater	0.68%	9,500,000
Lakes	0.01%	125,000
Soils	0.005%	65,000
Atmosphere	0.001%	13,000
Rivers	0.0001%	1,700
Living Organisms	0.00004%	600
TOTAL	**100.00%**	**1,408,700,000**

beaker. The oceans would contribute the vast majority of the 1,000 milliliters. In this comparison, the lakes and rivers would contribute just about one drop, and the atmosphere would be a very small part of a drop.

Of course, Earth has much more water than 1,000 milliliters. Earth's living organisms, the smallest reservoir in the Water Reservoir table, contains 600 cubic kilometers of water. One cubic kilometer fills a cube one kilometer high, one kilometer wide, and one kilometer deep. One cubic kilometer of water equals 260,000,000,000 gallons, enough water to fill 100 domed stadiums. This means that the water in all Earth's plants and animals would fill 60,000 domed stadiums. So, we're talking about a lot of water even in the smallest reservoir of Earth's water system.

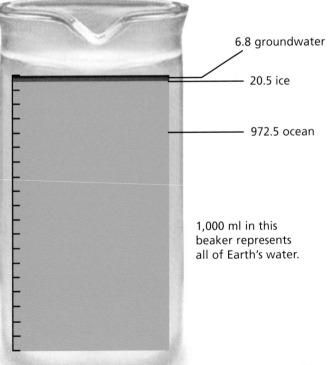

0.01 atmosphere
0.1 lakes & rivers

6.8 groundwater

20.5 ice

972.5 ocean

1,000 ml in this beaker represents all of Earth's water.

The Water Cycle

If water just stayed in the reservoirs, we would have a "water hanging out" thing on planet Earth. Instead, Earth features the famous water cycle. Water constantly moves from one reservoir to another. It evaporates from the ocean into the gas state. In the sky, it forms clouds, and then precipitates as rain back into the ocean and onto the land. If the water gets very cold, it freezes, forming snow and ice. It can then melt, and flow as liquid water on the surface or under the ground. Over the course of time, a water molecule changes both its physical state (gas, solid, liquid) and its physical location (ocean, atmosphere, glacier, river).

The Water Cycle illustration indicates the amounts of water that move in a year from one reservoir to another. Each unit is equal to 1,000 cubic kilometers of water (enough to fill one hundred thousand domed stadiums).

Check out how much water leaves the ocean each year. 434 units evaporate from the ocean each year. However, 398 of those units return directly to the ocean as precipitation (rain on the ocean). The remaining 36 units get carried in clouds over to the land, where they fall to the ground as rain and snow.

If this water did not return to the ocean, then the ocean would keep on losing water. However, that is not what happens. Over the course of a year, 36 units of water flow from the land into the ocean. As a result, just as much water enters the ocean as leaves it. The total volume of the ocean does not change.

Do you think the atmosphere loses or gains water over the course of a year? Check out the math, and confirm for yourself that the amount of water entering the atmosphere equals the amount of water leaving the atmosphere.

From a long-term global perspective, we see that the same water molecules are used over and over again. The hydrosphere, planet Earth's water system, is a closed system. No new water enters the hydrosphere. No used up water leaves the hydrosphere. The same water keeps moving from one reservoir to another, going round and round, leading to the name we give this phenomenon—the Water Cycle. The water cycle is another reason that people often find themselves muttering, "matter cycles, matter cycles, matter cycles."

To sum up, Earth's liquid stuff exists in reservoirs that are connected through the water cycle. These water reservoirs have different locations, physical states, and amounts. Even though water constantly leaves and enters them, these reservoirs tend to keep the same amount over the course of a year.

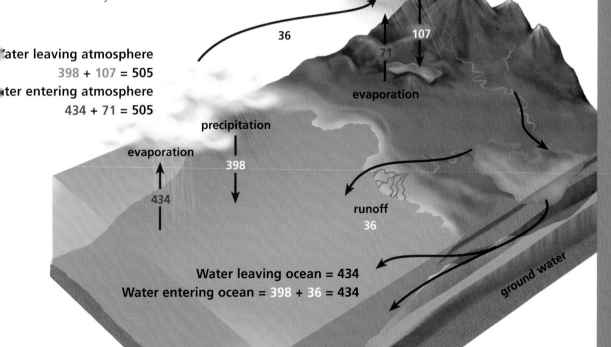

precipitation

36

107

Water leaving atmosphere
398 + 107 = 505

Water entering atmosphere
434 + 71 = 505

71

evaporation

precipitation

evaporation

398

434

runoff
36

Water leaving ocean = 434
Water entering ocean = 398 + 36 = 434

ground water

Here is another way to understand the water cycle. Think about one of our ancestors who lived in Africa a hundred thousand years ago. Or think about a dinosaur that lived 70 million years ago. Or consider a buffalo that roamed the American Midwest long before the arrival of humans. No matter which you choose to bring to mind, that organism drank water throughout its life. This water was present in every drink and in every grain, fish, or flesh that it consumed. The water molecules became part of that organism's body, and then flowed back into the world as blood, sweat, urine, and exhaled water vapor.

Now, fill a glass with water. This glass that you hold in your hand today has more than ten million water molecules that once passed through the body of the buffalo, more than ten million water molecules that passed through the dinosaur, and more than ten million water molecules that passed through one of our African ancestors! The water that we drink intimately connects us with the living beings that inhabited the planet before us, that inhabit Earth today, and that will inhabit it in the future.

BIG IDEA

The water that we drink connects us intimately with the living beings that inhabited the planet before us, that inhabit Earth today, and that will inhabit it in the future.

Earth's Gas Stuff

Earth's atmosphere is a very thin layer of air that protects and sustains us. At the top of tall mountains, most of us experience problems breathing due to the thinning of Earth's atmosphere. The higher we go, the fewer the gas atoms in the atmosphere, and the more the air resembles the emptiness of outer space.

BIG IDEA

The atmosphere is the most sensitive and changeable of Earth's spheres.

Compared to the geosphere and the hydrosphere, the atmosphere is the most sensitive and changeable of Earth's "spheres." It can change quickly because it is comparatively very small. In terms of mass, there is a million times more solid Earth stuff than its gas stuff. Therefore, if a small part of Earth's solid stuff changes to gas and enters the air, it can have a major effect on the atmosphere.

Nitrogen accounts for almost four fifths (78%) of the gas in the atmosphere. Oxygen at 21% accounts for almost all the rest. Other gases in the atmosphere are present in much smaller amounts, with carbon dioxide at about 0.04%. As we all experience, the atmosphere also has varying amounts of water vapor, depending on the location and the weather at any particular time. The same volume of warm air above a tropical rainforest can contain a hundred times more water than the cold, dry air over the Antarctic.

I hope you will not be surprised that the nitrogen, oxygen, and carbon located in Earth's atmosphere each participate in a matter cycle. By now, you should expect that matter on Earth is used over and over again. Everything on the planet is made of atoms, and these atoms on Earth are neither created nor destroyed. The same atoms keep combining, separating, and combining again with each other.

We will focus here on one of Earth's most important cycles, the carbon cycle. Since all Earth's organisms are carbon-based life forms, we should pay careful attention to the carbon cycle. Plants and animals actively participate in this cycle by taking carbon dioxide out of the atmosphere and putting it back into the atmosphere. Every year humans currently add eight billion extra tons of carbon into the atmosphere by burning fossil fuels and forests.

The Carbon Cycle

The carbon cycle is harder to understand than the water cycle. With the water cycle, we are always talking about the same molecule (H_2O). In going through the water cycle, these H_2O molecules change in their physical location and in their physical state (gas, liquid, and solid). In the carbon cycle, the carbon atoms change their location and physical state, but they also change which atoms they connect with. Unlike the water cycle, the molecules change.

Carbon in the atmosphere is mostly present as the gas carbon dioxide. In living and decaying matter, carbon is present as carbohydrates and protein. In these molecules, it bonds with oxygen, hydrogen, and other elements in a huge number of different chemicals. In the ocean, it is present mostly as bicarbonate salts (bicarbonate is a combination of carbon, oxygen, and hydrogen that is also commonly found on kitchen shelves in the form of baking soda). With the carbon cycle, we see the same carbon atoms changing their chemical partners as well as their physical location and physical state (gas, liquid, and solid) as they flow from one reservoir to another.

carbon dioxide

bicarbonate salts

protein

BIG IDEA

In the carbon cycle, the molecules change.

The carbon cycle illustration and table show five major carbon reservoirs on Earth. These are the Atmosphere, Biomass, Ocean, Sedimentary Rocks, and Fossil Fuels. The numbers next to the arrows represent the rate (in billions of tons per year) at which carbon enters and leaves each of those reservoirs. There is some uncertainty in the exact value of these numbers, but the relative amounts are correct.

Carbon Reservoirs & The Atmosphere				
RESERVOIR	FORM OF CARBON	AMOUNT OF CARBON	FLOW RATE WITH ATMOSPHERE	HUMAN EFFECTS ON ATMOSPHERE
Atmosphere	Carbon Dioxide (gas)	760 gigatons*		Greenhouse gases are increasing.
Biomass	Sugar, Cellulose, Protein, etc. (solid, dissolved)	2,000 gigatons	Per year, about 110 gigatons flow in each direction.	Burning forests release about 1 gigaton per year.
Sedimentary Rock	Carbonates (solid)	50,000,000 gigatons	About 0.05 gigatons per year	Negligible
Oceans	Mostly dissolved bicarbonate salts	39,000 gigatons	About 90 gigatons per year; the ocean is currently absorbing more than it releases.	Negligible
Fossil Fuels	Methane (gas), Petroleum (liquid), Coal (solid)	5,000 gigatons	About 7 gigatons per year through burning oil, coal, and methane.	About 7 gigatons per year above natural background rate through burning oil, coal, and methane.

*1 gigaton = 1 billion tons

It is easiest to understand the carbon cycle by exploring how each of the different reservoirs interacts with the atmosphere. We will examine how the atmosphere interacts with life, rocks, oceans, and fossil fuels. The atmosphere contains 760 billion tons of carbon (amount as of 2005), almost all of it present as carbon dioxide. This CO_2 currently makes up 0.038% of the atmosphere, a small percentage but essential for life as we know it.

The most famous part of the carbon cycle involves life. Organisms that perform photosynthesis use carbon dioxide gas from the atmosphere to make sugar. Each year, photosynthesis removes about one seventh of the carbon from the atmosphere. The atmosphere still has carbon because organisms use that carbon for energy. As a result, the carbon returns to the atmosphere, again in the form of carbon dioxide. This internal burning of carbon balances photosynthesis, so the amount of carbon in the atmosphere and in living organisms tends to remain the same.

When we think about life, we usually focus on animals. In the case of the carbon cycle, most of the carbon in living organisms is actually located in plants and decaying soil material. This organic carbon reservoir, called **Biomass**, has about four times as much carbon as the atmosphere. The carbon is chemically in the form of organic molecules such as sugars, starches, and proteins.

The oceans are a very significant reservoir in the carbon cycle, containing about 50 times more carbon than the atmosphere. This ocean carbon is present mostly as dissolved bicarbonate salt. The annual rate at which atmospheric carbon enters and leaves the ocean is similar to

Carbon Cycle

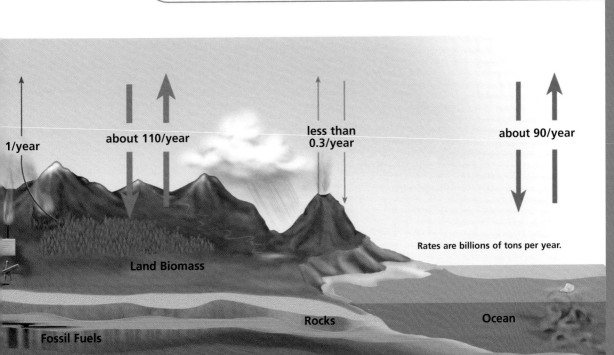

1/year

about 110/year

less than 0.3/year

about 90/year

Rates are billions of tons per year.

Land Biomass

Rocks

Ocean

Fossil Fuels

the rate of exchange with land biomass. In other words, about every seven years all the carbon in the atmosphere will leave it and become part of the ocean. Similarly, about every seven years approximately the same amount will leave the ocean and return to the atmosphere.

Rocks contain the vast majority of Earth's surface carbon, more than 50,000 times as much as the atmosphere. However, this huge store of carbon interacts with the atmosphere at a much slower rate. In one direction, a process called weathering removes carbon from the atmosphere. In the other direction, volcanoes and other processes return the carbon from Earth's interior to the atmosphere. We met this part of the carbon cycle when we explored the rock cycle.

A Closed System For Matter

Our planet has been circling the Sun for more than four billion years. During those billions of years, the matter on our planet keeps changing its form. Water evaporates from the ocean, goes into the clouds, and falls as snow and rain. Rocks get broken down into dirt that is washed as sediment into rivers. Plants take carbon dioxide gas from the atmosphere, and convert it into solid sugars and starches. Why doesn't all the ocean water turn into mountain snow, or all the rocks turn into sediment, or all the atmospheric carbon dioxide turn into sugar?

Earth still has oceans, mountains, and atmospheric carbon dioxide because they are part of cycles — the water cycle, the rock cycle, and the carbon cycle. Water flows in rivers back to the oceans; buried sediments reach the surface again through volcanoes; and animals chemically change sugars into carbon dioxide that goes back into the atmosphere.

Earth is a recycling planet. Essentially all the matter on Earth has been here since the planet was formed. We don't get new matter; old matter does not go away into outer space. The same matter keeps getting used over and over again. From a systems point of view, we say that Earth is a closed system with respect to matter. Matter cycles, matter cycles, matter cycles.

Matter Cycles

Each of the elements that is vital for life exists on Earth in a closed loop of cyclical changes. From a systems point of view, Earth is essentially a closed system with respect to matter.

STOP & THINK

You probably use reading strategies without even being aware of them. For example, I bet there are times when you are reading and you know that you are just saying the words to yourself, without really understanding what the sentence or paragraph means. That self-awareness is actually part of a good reading strategy. But you need to do something when you realize that you have not understood what you read.

That self-awareness motivates successful readers to go back and try to understand what they did not get the first time around. They may read the section again, look at illustrations, check an earlier page to clarify a question, look up a word in a dictionary, or talk with someone about the reading.

Here is a different strategy that also helps you think about what you are reading. This strategy works especially well when you start a new chapter. First look over the chapter as a kind of preview. Look at the chapter title, section headings, illustrations, and highlighted words. Then make a chart such as the one below, and fill out the first three rows.

What I know I know that is in the chapter.	
What I think I know that is in the chapter.	
What I think I will learn by reading this chapter.	
What I know I learned by reading this chapter.	

As you read, think about what you wrote and what are the new things that you are learning. After you finish the chapter, look over the chart and compare what you know now to what you knew before you read the chapter. Write what you know you learned by reading the chapter.

Here comes Chapter 8, a very good place to start with this reading strategy.

ENERGY ON EARTH

The Goldilocks Planet

Back in Chapter 2, we learned about systems thinking as a way to understand any system, especially complicated ones like planet Earth. We said that three systems questions often help us analyze the system that we are exploring. When we looked at Earth's matter, we mostly used the first systems question, "What are the parts of the system?"

We examined Earth's solid, liquid, and gas parts and discovered that they all participated in cycles. We concluded that matter on planet Earth cycles, that Earth is essentially a closed system for matter.

What if we asked the same system question about Earth's energy? Looking for Earth's energy "parts," we might run around measuring the wind, hot springs, volcanoes, waterfalls, and humans making fires. However, if we take a break and relax on the beach, we would realize that we had ignored Earth's most important source of energy.

It's way out there. It's not one of Earth's parts. It provides our planet with 10,000 times more energy than all our societies consume. Of course, it's the Sun. To understand energy in the Earth system, we need

BIG IDEA

Earth is a solar planet. The Sun keeps our planet warm and sustains life.

to focus on a different systems question. Instead of looking at the parts of the Earth system, we need to ask the third system question—how is Earth itself part of larger systems?

And the answer is as simple as the question—Earth is part of the solar system. The Sun provides virtually all the energy to keep our planet warm and sustain life.

Since our solar system has many other planets, we also discover how important it is to be close to the Sun, but not too close. When the planets first formed, the areas closer to the Sun were too hot for anything but rocky materials to solidify. So these inner planets (Mercury, Venus, Earth, and Mars) are mostly rock. In contrast, the outer planets (such as Jupiter and Saturn) were cool enough to keep gases such as methane and ammonia. These planets became very large, consisting mostly of atmospheres containing these and other gases.

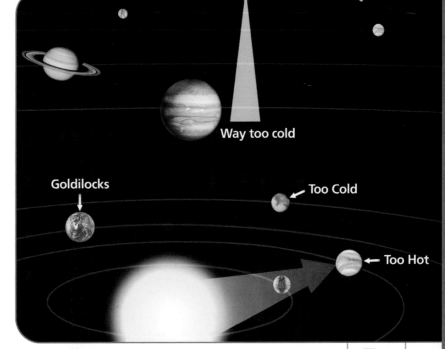

Some people have called this third planet from the Sun, the Goldilocks planet. In the children's story involving the three bears, Goldilocks found the chair that was not too big or not too small. She ate the porridge that was not too hot or not too cold. Earth is not too close to the Sun, not too far, not too hot, and not too cold. Earth is just right.

An Open System

Imagine what would happen if the Sun stopped shining! Goldilocks would become a dark, super-frozen wasteland.

This nightmare emphasizes the crucial role of solar energy. Our planet relies on a constant input of energy from the Sun. Earth receives an inflow of solar energy that is more than 10,000 times the amount of energy consumed by all human societies. This constant flow of solar energy into the planet provides virtually all the energy to keep our planet warm and make life possible

If Earth kept all that energy, it would become so hot that it would just boil away. But energy does not stay in any one place. Energy flows away from Earth as heat that radiates to outer space. The amount of energy going from Earth to outer space equals the amount of energy flowing in from the Sun.

Note the difference between Earth's matter and Earth's energy. With respect to matter, Earth is a closed system. Matter does not enter or leave. With respect to energy, Earth is an open system. Sunlight energy flows in, and heat energy escapes.

Energy Flows

The functioning of our planet relies on a constant input of energy from the Sun. This energy leaves Earth in the form of heat flowing to outer space. From a systems point of view, Earth is an open system with respect to energy.

Conduction

Since energy never changes in amount, you might think that it does not live up to its name. However, energy is not dull. Energy is, well, energetic. It changes very readily, and can move rapidly from one place to another.

If we heat one end of a metal object, such as a nail, we discover that the other end gets hot very quickly. When we add energy to an object, the extra energy makes the atoms move faster. In some materials, such as metals, the rapidly moving atoms cause their neighboring atoms to move faster. In turn, these atoms cause their neighboring atoms to move faster. The faster the atoms move, the higher the temperature. In this way, heat energy added at one end of an object causes the temperature at the other end to increase.

When heat moves this way, we call it **conduction**. The heat energy is conducted along the nail because the extra jiggling of the atoms rapidly passes along the length of the object. The atoms themselves do not move from one end to the other. Their increased jiggling is passed from one end to the other.

Electromagnetic Radiation

Energy can travel a second way. You experience this way that energy moves every time that you feel the Sun's energy. No atoms are moving 93 million miles through empty space to bring the Sun's energy to Earth. Instead, heat and light travel from the Sun to Earth as invisible, speeding waves.

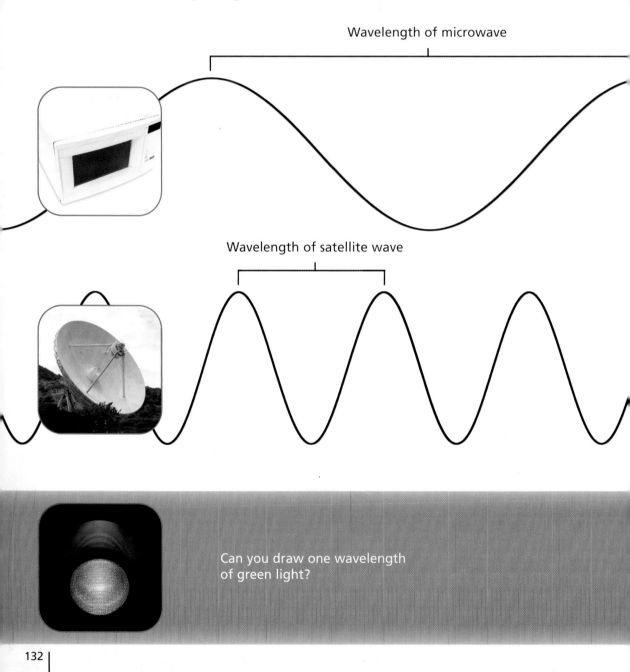

Wavelength of microwave

Wavelength of satellite wave

Can you draw one wavelength of green light?

How fast do these waves of heat and light energy travel? I bet you know the answer. They travel at the speed of light. That is our old friend c, from the Einstein $E = mc^2$ equation. In other words, light and heat waves travel as fast as anything can travel.

Other forms of energy also travel as waves moving at the speed of light. These include radio waves going from a broadcast station through the air to people's radios. They also include microwaves traveling inside our ovens.

The feature that makes these waves different from each other is their wavelength. Waves of green light have a different wavelength than radio waves, whose waves have a different wavelength than microwaves.

Microwave radiation in an oven has a wavelength of about 12 cm. The previous page shows how that wave would appear. In contrast, a communications satellite may broadcast at a wavelength of 4 cm, as shown in the illustration. Green light has a much shorter wavelength of about 0.00005 cm. If you use an electron microscope to examine the pattern that Emiko Paul (this book's illustrator) has drawn for a wave of green light, you will see that she has drawn 500,000 wavelengths!

I try to avoid using scary sounding scientific words in this book. Well, don't freak out, but to explain solar energy and heat radiating, I need to use the words "electromagnetic radiation" and "electromagnetic spectrum."

Many very familiar forms of energy are electromagnetic in nature. Examples include green light, red light, microwaves, radio waves, ultraviolet light, and X-rays. Scientists call them electromagnetic because, guess what, they have electrical and magnetic properties. Equally important, they all travel at the speed of light (in other words, as fast as anything can go), do not lose energy as they travel (even over huge distances, such as from the Sun to Earth), and they travel as waves.

X-RAY
Wavelength ranges from 10^{-9} to 10^{-6} cm

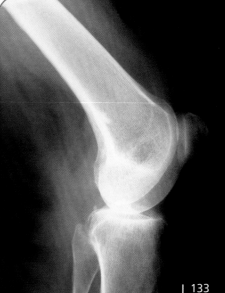

When energy moves that way, scientists call it **electromagnetic radiation**. Some of these forms of energy even have wave or ray right in their name. The broad range from electromagnetic waves with incredibly tiny wavelengths to much longer electromagnetic waves is called the **electromagnetic spectrum**.

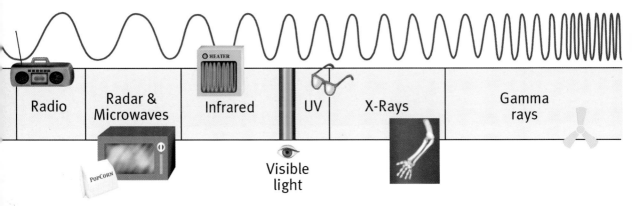

| Radio | Radar & Microwaves | Infrared | UV | X-Rays | Gamma rays |

Visible light

The electromagnetic spectrum (meaning a broad range going from one end to the other) includes electromagnetic waves that differ by more than a million times in the size of their wavelengths. An x-ray may have a wavelength that is a thousand times shorter than green light which itself may have a wavelength ten thousand times shorter than a radio wave.

Energy From The Sun

The Sun is not boring. It doesn't give off just one wavelength. It radiates energy across a fairly broad range of wavelengths. You know this because you have seen rainbows, natural examples where some of the Sun's light separates into its different wavelengths. The shorter waves (which we see as blue colors) appear at the bottom and the longer waves (red colors) appear at the top.

The Sun radiates about half of its energy in the visible part of the electromagnetic spectrum. In other words, we see half of the Sun's radiant energy ranging from shorter wavelengths, that we see as violet, to wavelengths about twice as long, that we see as red. The Sun emits 40% of its energy in the infrared (IR) region (longer than red wavelengths which some animals, such as rattlesnakes, can see). It also emits 10% of its radiation as ultraviolet (UV) rays (shorter than violet which some animals, such as bees, can see).

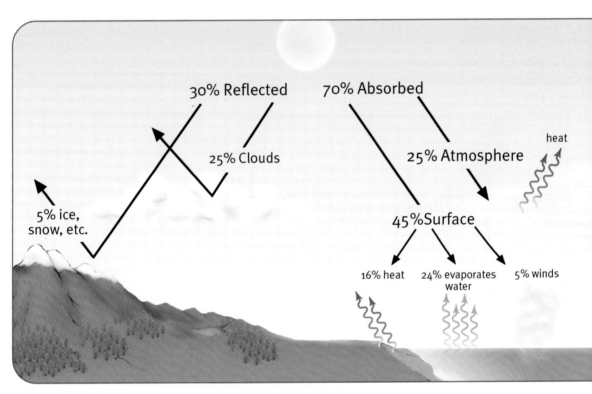

Check out what happens to the solar energy that reaches Earth. About 30% is immediately reflected back as light to outer space. Most of this light bounces off the clouds and never reaches the surface. Some of it reaches the surface, but bounces off snow and water, and then leaves the Earth system in the form of light. Photos of Earth from space capture this reflected light to show us how our planet appears.

The remaining 70% of the sunlight that reaches Earth is absorbed. As shown in the illustration, this absorption occurs in a number of ways. Most of it is absorbed by solid materials and water, and is immediately converted to heat. We all experience this energy change when sunlight

warms our bodies. What we don't consciously experience is that this heat energy radiates from our bodies. Any material that is heated by the Sun will then radiate heat outwards. Sometimes we see this heat as in the shimmering waves of air above a hot pavement. Eventually that heat radiates through the atmosphere and leaves planet Earth by flowing to outer space.

A large amount of the solar energy evaporates water, thereby powering the water cycle. Water absorbs this energy as it changes from the liquid state to the gas state. Water vapor then leaves the oceans and enters the atmosphere. However, when this water vapor condenses back to the liquid state (rain), the same amount of energy is released in this condensation process as the amount that was absorbed in the evaporation. This energy is now released as heat that escapes to the atmosphere and eventually to outer space. So, even the sunlight that powers the water cycle also eventually leaves Earth in the form of heat.

The same fate awaits the Sun's energy that is initially converted to the moving energy of wind, waves and currents. For example, the wind rubs against a cliff and some of its energy changes to heat.

As long as energy is not changing into mass (or vice versa), it does not increase or decrease in amount. Another key characteristic is that energy changes form, eventually changing to heat energy. All the solar energy that is absorbed on Earth eventually changes to heat energy that radiates to outer space.

Heat radiates to the atmosphere, and eventually to outer space.

The Greenhouse Effect

You may have heard about Earth's famous greenhouse effect. Now that we have explored the electromagnetic spectrum and how the Sun's energy heats our planet, we can understand the greenhouse effect, and why it is important.

Light from the Sun shines on water, rocks, soil, sand, buildings, roads, clouds, and organisms. What happens to a rock, or any other object, when light rays shine on them? The energy from the light makes the rock molecules move faster. In other words, the rock becomes warmer. If something feels warm to us, that means its molecules have more energy, and are moving faster. The faster the molecules move, the higher is the temperature of the rock.

Do warm objects stay warm? No, they tend to get colder. Remember, energy does not tend to stay in one place. A hot object, such as a rock in the Sun, gives off some of its energy as electromagnetic rays. These are infrared waves (longer than red) that carry heat away from the rock. When you feel heat from a fire, or from any other hot object that you are not physically touching, you are generally experiencing infrared heat rays that have radiated to you from the fire or the hot object.

Infrared rays from all over the planet radiate out to the atmosphere. The energy started as visible light from the Sun that passed right through the atmosphere, crashed into objects and heated them. This energy then travels from the objects in the form of longer wavelength infrared (IR) radiation.

Unlike the shorter wavelength visible light, this infrared radiation does not just pass through the atmosphere. Certain gases in Earth's atmosphere absorb the radiated heat energy. These atmospheric greenhouse gases (mostly water vapor and carbon dioxide) then radiate that heat energy so that half of it returns to Earth. This heat is absorbed before being radiated back out again to the atmosphere. The net result is that heat energy stays longer within the Earth system.

Water vapor and carbon dioxide are called greenhouse gases because they let light rays pass through, but they absorb heat rays. Most of the molecules in the atmosphere (oxygen and nitrogen) are not greenhouse gases. These molecules do not interact with either the sunlight entering or the heat escaping the planet.

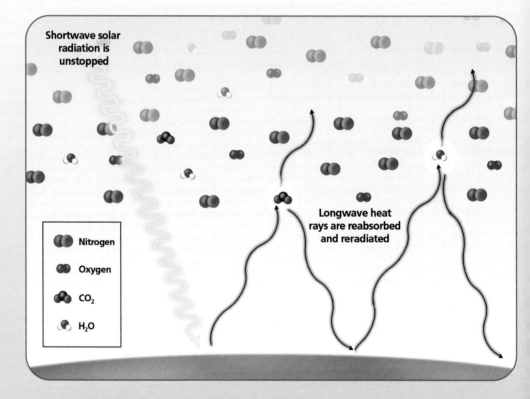

We are very lucky that Earth has this greenhouse effect, keeping the heat longer within the Earth system. As a result, Earth is about 33 degrees Celsius (60 degrees Fahrenheit) warmer than it would be in the absence of the greenhouse effect. Without the greenhouse gases in the atmosphere, Earth's average temperature would be well below the freezing point of water. It would be colder than the ice ages that Earth has experienced.

Earth's Internal Energy

Until now we have emphasized that the Sun provides virtually all the energy for planet Earth. This solar radiation keeps Earth warm, powers the wind, drives the water cycle, and provides the energy for almost all Earth's creatures.

In the previous chapter, we explored a different kind of energy and some important roles that it plays in the Earth system. We saw Africa and South America being dragged apart, while the Indian subcontinent traveled 4,000 miles and crashed into Asia. What energy source provides the power to move continents? Even the Sun, our greatest energy source, does not move continents.

Volcanoes, earthquakes, geysers, and hot springs provide the answer. Earth's interior is hot enough to melt rocks and metal. This heat energy constantly moves as it slowly travels from the interior to the cooler surface. The hottest material deep in Earth's interior slowly rises toward the surface, and cooler material sinks toward the interior. This heat flow cause Earth's plates to move (remember the plates?) with their resulting earthquakes, volcanoes, and moving continents.

When Earth first formed, the heat was so great that the entire planet consisted of melted rock/metal. Since that time, it has been cooling with heat rising to the surface and radiating to outer space. In addition, new heat is continually being generated inside the Earth. Our planet contains many radioactive elements that break down, and release heat in this decay process. This heat from radioactive decay plus the

heat remaining from Earth's formation provide the power to move the plates, drag continents apart, or crash them into each other.

How large is this energy source that can move continents, blow the top off Mount St. Helens, and create mountains such as Everest? This chart compares all of Earth's energy flows. If we assign the value of 1.0 to the amount of energy that human societies consume, then the Moon provides about a quarter that amount through its effect on the oceans and tides. Earth's internal energy flow is 2.5 times as large, and the Sun provides 10,000 times that amount.

Comparing Amounts of Energy	
TYPE OF ENERGY	RELATIVE AMOUNT
Human Society	1.0
Tidal	.25
Internal	2.5
Solar	10,000

How can something that seems so weak have such large effects? A Chinese saying provides an important clue: "The journey of a thousand miles begins with a single step." The flow of internal energy moves the plates at rates of only centimeters per year. Yet, over hundreds of millions of years, those centimeters add up to thousands of kilometers.

So although Earth's internal geothermal energy contributes very little energy compared to the Sun, it is a very important part of Earth's energy budget. Tyler Volk, an Earth Systems

BIG IDEA

Only Earth's internal energy can make mountains out of molehills.

scientist at New York University, has written that while the energy from the Sun through falling rain and blowing wind can make molehills out of mountains, only Earth's internal energy can make mountains out of molehills.

Earth's Energy Budget

We can also think about Earth's energy in terms of a budget. Just like a family budget or a government budget, in any particular time period, a certain amount comes in and a certain amount goes out. A family or a company or a government can borrow money so they can send out more than they take in. Earth is different. Earth has a balanced energy budget.

The amount of energy that flows out as heat from Earth's surface and atmosphere to outer space is exactly equal to the amount of energy that reaches the surface and atmosphere. As we have seen, solar radiation accounts for the vast majority of that energy. A much smaller, but very important, amount comes from the interior. Of course, at any given moment more energy could be flowing in than is flowing out. But over the course of a year or longer, this balances and the amount of energy flowing out equals the amount of energy flowing in.

Earth's "matter budget" would look very different. Essentially nothing comes in and nothing goes out. The same stuff keeps getting used over and over. In comparing matter and energy, we say that Earth is a closed system for matter and an open system for energy.

The greenhouse effect adds an important feature to Earth's energy budget. Certain gases in the atmosphere (most importantly, water vapor and carbon dioxide) slow down the rate at which heat escapes from the Earth system. In effect, these gases make the heat stay longer within the Earth system.

People often mistakenly think that the greenhouse effect is a bad thing, that it is something that humans cause. Earth's greenhouse effect has helped make temperatures on the planet comfortable for life for billions of years. It started long before anything resembling humans appeared on the scene.

> Earth's temperature is increasing. The cause appears to be an increase greenhouse effect.

Year(s)	Greenhouse effect	Average Earth temperature
1860 - 1890	32° C??	About 14.6 °C
1960 - 1990	32.5 °C??	About 15.1 °C
2004	33 °C??	About 15.5 °C

However, you can have too much of a good thing. Humans are currently adding greenhouse gases to the atmosphere. By doing that, we are changing Earth's energy budget. We are making the heat energy stay in the Earth system even longer than it would have. This is the issue of Global Climate Change that we will discuss in the book's last chapter.

The main reason we care about Earth's energy budget and the planet's climate is that we and many other creatures live here. The next chapter explores the system of life on planet Earth, including us.

STOP & DO

In this chapter, we discussed two ways that heat moves. If we heat an end of an iron nail, the other end gets hot because of conduction. The jiggling motion of the atoms quickly passes along the length of the nail (page 131). Heat also travels from objects as electromagnetic radiation (page 137). We feel warmth from a rock or a fire because infrared radiation travels from the object.

Neither conduction nor radiation involves the molecules traveling and bringing the heat energy with them. In **convection**, a third way that heat travels, the "hot molecules" move. Convection happens when liquids and gases are heated. Molecules move upward from the heated area. In the cooler areas, molecules move downwards. Convection sets up a circular flow that rapidly transports the heat.

Convection is a very important way that heat moves in the Earth system. Convection moves heat within Earth's interior, and plays important roles in plate tectonics. Convection moves heat in Earth's atmosphere, and plays important roles in weather and climate.

You can use food dyes and water to visualize convection. Set up a pie dish so it rests securely on three, inverted, 6-ounce cups. Place water about five centimeters deep in the pie dish. Insert a fourth cup filled with room temperature water, facing upwards, under the center of the dish.

Carefully place a drop of food dye in the bottom, center of the dish. Observe how it diffuses in the water. After a while, you can stir the water and let it settle.

Go to next page ...

STOP & DO
CONTINUED

This is not convection; it is the control. Now, VERY CAREFULLY replace the center cup with a cup filled with very hot water. Repeat putting a drop in the bottom center of the dish. Watch how it moves. Stir, let settle, and try another drop halfway to an edge from the center. Watch how it moves.

Experiment with different temperatures and dye locations. Look for patterns of dye moving upwards, downwards, and horizontally. The Chapter 8 section of the guidetoscience website has more information about convection.

This activity is summarized from the Great Explorations in Math and Science (GEMS) teacher's guide entitled, *Convection: A Current Event*, ©1988 by the Regents of the University of California, and used with permission.

LIFE ON EARTH

A Networked System

Way, way back in the first two chapters, we started this book by discussing photosynthesis. Now, more than 100 pages later, I am sure you still remember that plants take energy from the Sun and carbon dioxide from the air to make sugar. In this process, they also release oxygen to the atmosphere.

Almost all Earth organisms depend on photosynthesis. They use the sugars for fuel and to make the parts of their bodies. Many of them need to breathe the oxygen in the air.

The organisms that do photosynthesis depend on other organisms to return the carbon to the atmosphere as carbon dioxide that they can use again in photosynthesis. Plants also often rely on animals for pollination or for spreading seeds. They also depend on small creatures in the ground to create rich soil from dead waste.

Earth is unique in the solar system in being a planet of life.

In these and many other ways, Earth's organisms form a vast web of interconnections. Every organism depends on and significantly affects many other organisms. Not only do organisms form an interconnected web among themselves, they also participate actively in Earth's cycles of matter and flows of energy. In systems language, we say that Earth is a networked system with respect to life.

We humans depend on the web of life for the air that we breathe and the food that we eat. As our numbers have greatly increased and our technologies have changed virtually every part of the globe, we have become a very important part of this web of life.

As far as we know, Earth is unique in the solar system in being a planet of life. Living creatures have dwelled here for almost four billion years. Life has become such an important part of our planet that Earth without life simply would not be Earth.

A vast and intricate network of relationships connects all Earth's organisms with each other, and with the cycles of matter and the flows of energy. From a systems point of view, Earth is a networked system with respect to life.

Who Is In The Web?

When we investigated Earth's matter, we asked the first systems question: "What are the parts of the system?" In looking at Earth's energy, we focused on the third systems question: "How is the system itself part of larger systems?" In exploring the system of life on Earth, we are going to focus on the second system question: "How does the system function as a whole?" What is this web of life and how does it work?

Earth has four kinds of stuff—solid, liquid, gas, and living. In comparison with Earth's living matter, there is four thousand times more gas stuff, one million times more liquid stuff, and four billion times more solid Earth material. Yet, despite its small amount, life plays very important roles on our planet.

With respect to mass, almost all of Earth's living stuff is in the form of plant matter. All animal life adds up to only 1% of Earth's **biomass**. Trees and decaying plant matter account for almost all the mass of Earth's living stuff.

The closer you get to the equator, the more trees there are. The climate is better for trees, and there is a lot more land near the equator than near the poles. As a result, tropical forests account for about 40% of Earth's total biomass. This is one reason why many people are concerned about the high rate at which tropical forests are being destroyed. If we burned all of Earth's trees, that would double the amount of carbon in the atmosphere.

BIG IDEA

We know the number of atoms in the universe better than we know the number of species on our planet.

Another important way to understand Earth's life is in term of the kinds of organisms that exist rather than their mass. The word **biodiversity** refers to the number and kinds of different organisms. We know very little about Earth's biodiversity. We have a more accurate scientific estimate of the number of atoms in the universe than we do of the number of different species on our planet.

Scientists have currently named and catalogued about 1,500,000 different species of organisms. The estimates of the total number range from five million to 30 million or even more. Of the 1.5 million that have been described, all that we know about the majority of these is what they look like, and where a few specimens were obtained.

Where is this biodiversity located? Here, too, the tropical forests play a major role. Biologist E. O. Wilson once found as many different kinds of ants on one tree in Peru as exists in all the British Isles. An area in Indonesia totaling approximately 25 acres contained as many different tree species as are native to all of North America. A naturalist in 1875 described 700 species of butterflies within an hour walk of a town on the Amazon River. In contrast, all of Europe has only 321 different butterfly species.

Unfortunately, we are losing much of this biodiversity. Each year, increasing populations and economic development destroy large areas of wild rainforest. This wealth of biodiversity may disappear before we even know what we have lost forever.

All of Europe's Butterflies

South American
BUTTERFLIES Vol. III

South American
BUTTERFLIES Vol. IV

South American
BUTTERFLIES Vol. VIII

Breath Of Life

Into air

Oxygen

Water

Hydrogen

Carbohydrate
(fructose)

Carbon

Oxygen

Carbon
Dioxide

Earth's original atmosphere had no oxygen gas. The oxygen in our atmosphere came from photosynthesis.

For most of Earth's history, bacteria were the only organisms that inhabited the planet. They invented photosynthesis as a way to capture energy from sunlight, and to package that energy in chemical form as sugars. As you know, this photosynthesis also puts oxygen into the atmosphere.

In photosynthesis, the oxygen is actually a by-product. Sugars are carbohydrates (popularly abbreviated as "carbs"), meaning that they have carbon, hydrogen, and oxygen (the "ates" part of the word stands for oxygen). Carbon dioxide provides the carbon and the oxygen in carbohydrates. The hydrogen comes from water. When photosynthesis uses the hydrogen from water, the oxygen from the water molecules gets released into the atmosphere.

Organisms that perform photosynthesis take carbon dioxide from the atmosphere and pump oxygen into the air. So, does that mean all the carbon dioxide should disappear from the atmosphere and the oxygen should keep increasing?

No way. To get energy, organisms (plants, bacteria, animals, and fungi) internally burn sugars back into carbon dioxide gas. This reaction, the opposite of photosynthesis, is called respiration.

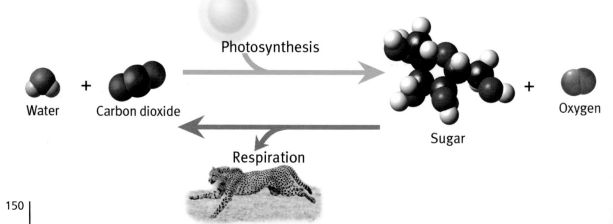

Water + Carbon dioxide → Photosynthesis → Sugar + Oxygen

Respiration

Organisms combine sugars with oxygen to form carbon dioxide and water. By burning the sugar, they release the stored chemical energy for their life processes.

Although we did not use the word, we did encounter respiration in the carbon cycle illustration from Chapter 7 (page 123). That illustration shows two arrows connecting Land Biomass with the Atmosphere. The arrow pointing downwards represents photosynthesis—plants and trees taking more than 100 billion tons of carbon out of the atmosphere each year and converting it into sugars. The solid arrow pointing upwards represents respiration— these plants, decomposers, and animals internally burning that sugar carbon and converting it back into carbon dioxide.

Ecosystems

We have discussed Earth's web of life in terms of the amount and kinds of living beings. However, we are still missing a very important part of understanding life on Earth. How it is organized?

Dr. Art is thrilled to report that the systems word is used in describing how living beings organize themselves in different places. We use the scientific term **ecosystem** to describe the organisms that live in a particular place, their relationships with each other, and their interactions with their physical environment. Hopefully, you have experienced different ecosystems such as a lake, meadow, creek, forest, coastal tide-pool, coral reef, or desert.

All the different ecosystems have a similar pattern of organization. They all require a source of energy, and a group of organisms that can capture that energy, and store it in chemical form. For the vast majority of ecosystems, the Sun provides the energy. Plant life, ranging from microscopic algae to towering redwood trees, captures the energy in sunlight and stores it as chemical energy in sugar molecules.

BIG IDEA

All the different ecosystems have a similar pattern of organization.

The organisms in an ecosystem that capture the energy are called producers (labeled P in the illustration below). All the other organisms in the ecosystem are called consumers because they depend either directly or indirectly on the producers for their food.

Animals are consumers, either eating plants (H, herbivores) or other animals (C, carnivores). Some animals, such as bears and humans, eat both plants and animals. In addition to the producers and consumers, a third group of organisms called decomposers (D) break down dead animals and plants.

Ecosystems, like other systems, can be described or investigated at many different levels. There are ecosystems within ecosystems within ecosystems. A meadow ecosystem includes plants, insects, gophers, snakes, deer, fungi, and bacteria. The forest in which the meadow is located is another ecosystem. An even larger ecosystem would be a

mountain containing the forest, meadow, and perhaps a lake. Earth's web of life is the sum total of all Earth's ecosystems.

In any ecosystem, the producers, consumers, and decomposers establish a network of feeding relationships called a food web. The same material keeps getting used over and over again as one organism eats another, and they all decompose back into the soil. Recycling is the ecosystem way of life.

Analyzing the energy flow through the ecosystem provides another perspective on its organization. The organisms that have the highest total energy flowing through them are the producers. All the biological energy that flows through the ecosystem's organisms must first be captured by these producers. In the course of living and reproducing, some of that energy escapes as heat to the atmosphere. The herbivores (cows, sheep, squirrels, etc.) that eat the producers spend a lot of energy in maintaining their body temperature, mating, eating and protecting themselves. This energy eventually escapes to the atmosphere as heat. Therefore there is less biological energy available to support the carnivores (snakes, owls, mountain lions, people) that eat the herbivores.

One result is that a typical land ecosystem will have five to ten times as much biomass in plant life than it will in herbivores. It will also support five to ten times as much biomass in herbivores as it will in carnivores. This feature is often portrayed as a pyramid showing the producers as the broad ecosystem base, with a narrower middle representing the herbivores, and a very narrow top representing the carnivores.

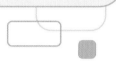

BIG IDEA

Recycling is the ecosystem way of life.

How Ecosystems Change

Think about the forest/meadow ecosystem shown on the previous pages. Imagine that a new disease kills all the rabbits. How would that affect the mouse population?

The mice might increase since there may be more plant food for them to eat. On the other hand, the hawks and foxes might eat more mice to replace the rabbits that they normally would have eaten. This could cause a decrease in the mouse population.

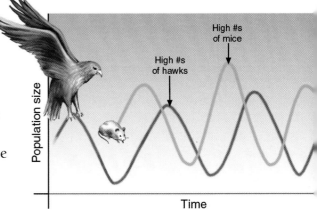

This type of question often occurs when we study a system. What happens when one of the parts changes? How do the parts connect with and influence each other?

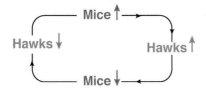

In general, the parts of a system connect with and influence each other in two different ways. We call these balancing feedback loops and reinforcing feedback loops.

A balancing feedback loop—surprise!—tends to keep things in balance. Predators and prey exist in a balancing feedback loop. If a mouse population increases, the hawks tend to increase since they have more mice to eat. The increase in hawks then reduces the mouse population, serving to balance the initial increase in mice. Check out the graph above to see how changes in one population cause changes in the other population.

Balancing feedback loops are very common. A thermostat is an example of a balancing feedback loop. A room gets too cold, triggering the thermostat to turn on the heater. When the room reaches the set temperature, the thermostat turns the heater off. The room temperature stays in balance, moving just a few degrees above and below the set temperature.

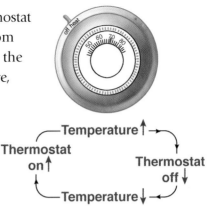

With a reinforcing feedback loop, a change in one direction causes more change in the same direction. Ten rabbits are brought to a new continent where they have abundant food and no natural predators. Each rabbit on average causes ten new babies so the population quickly becomes 110. Each of these results in ten new rabbits, a population of 110 + 1,100 = 1,210. This reinforcing feedback loop (more rabbits causes more babies causes more rabbits causes more babies) quickly results in a population explosion with millions of rabbits reproducing like rabbits all over Australia.

A microphone producing a loud, annoying, high-pitched squeal is another example of a reinforcing feedback loop. The microphone picks up a little bit of noise, feeds it into the amplifier which makes it louder, and then broadcasts the louder noise via the speakers. The microphone "hears" the louder noise, feeds it back into the amplifier, which then broadcasts the even louder noise through the speakers. This repeating loop of reinforcing feedback produces a very annoying, high-pitched microphone squeal.

Complicated systems such as ecosystems have many parts that connect with each other. A change in one part will cause changes in other parts. Some of the changes get balanced while others are reinforced. All these influences feed into each other, causing the whole system to change, often in unexpected ways. You may have experienced situations where simple actions cause unexpected results.

"Parachuting Cats Into Borneo" is a famous example. The World Health Organization (WHO) sprayed the insecticide DDT in Borneo in the 1950s in order to fight malaria, a disease spread by mosquitoes. The people lived in homes with thatched roofs. Suddenly, their roofs collapsed.

In addition to killing mosquitoes, the DDT killed parasitic wasps that preyed on caterpillars that ate the roof materials. Without the wasps, the caterpillars multiplied out of control and destroyed the roofs. Geckos, a native lizard, also died from eating DDT-poisoned insects. The dying geckos were caught and eaten by house cats, that then died from the DDT.

The death of the cats caused an increase in rats, which threatened to cause an outbreak of bubonic plague. WHO then parachuted cats into Borneo to try to control the rat population. They clearly did not have this in mind when they began spraying DDT.

We seem to keep needing to learn this lesson about the web of life. All the parts are connected via feedback loops. When we change the web of life, it is hard to predict the consequences. Unexpectedly, roofs may fall down...

... and rats may multiply out of control.

Since we don't want that to happen, let's learn some more about the science of life in the next chapter.

STOP & THINK

RAFT, one of my favorite literacy strategies, involves writing as well as reading. After you read a section or a chapter, design a way to explain the main ideas in an interesting written form such as a song, letter, commercial, poem, or short story.

RAFT stands for role, audience, format, and topic. I would rather call it TRAF because we should start with the topic. What are the main ideas that we learned? Once we know those, then we move on to developing a creative way to express those ideas for others.

If we want to do a RAFT after reading about photosynthesis, we would pick out the main ideas. Then we have to choose the role of the presenter, the audience receiving the presentation, and the form. The Table below has some examples.

Role	Audience	Format
Ray of light as a travel agent	Other light rays	Adventure commercial
Plant	Light rays	Love song
Carbon dioxide molecule	Himself/herself	Shakespeare speech about changes coming
Sugar molecule	Candy bar	Rap song about where it came from

Doing this by yourself could become boring. RAFT works best as a group activity. Try this for the chapter that you just finished. If you have enough people, designate a person or group to do a RAFT for each of the chapter's five sections. If you have enough for six groups, divide the "How Ecosystems Change" section into two parts, one for feedback loops, and one for cats from Borneo. Develop your RAFTs, and then perform them for the whole group.

As this activity illustrates, reading can be a social experience. Many of us think of reading as something we do by ourselves. As RAFT shows, we can have fun and learn more by sharing our reading experiences with others.

WHO WE ARE

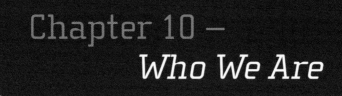

What Is Life?

In previous chapters, we have explored matter, energy, forces, the universe, and our beautiful home planet. We now turn our attention inward to ask a question that we humans have asked ourselves throughout history. Who are we?

The simplest answer to the "Who Are We?" question is: We are Earthlings, a form of life that is part of Earth's web of life. But what does it mean to be "a form of life?"

Consider the following things:

A lake – A building – A pine tree – A rock
Martin Luther King, Jr. – An ant – Yourself – The Sun
The Milky Way galaxy – Crystals hanging in a cave

The vast majority of people would agree that trees, ants, and human beings are alive. In contrast, most of us would say that a lake, a building, a rock, the Sun, cave crystals, Martin Luther King, and the Milky Way are not alive. Yet, despite the fact that we can generally classify objects into "alive" and "not alive," it is surprisingly difficult to write a simple definition of life.

Take the example of crystals hanging in a cave. Like us, they grow and change as they exchange matter and energy with their environment. A nonliving crystal even seems to reproduce, making accurate copies of itself. In a cave, for example, tiny crystal pieces break off, get stuck in new locations, and then grow to become large crystals.

Or consider a star. From our time frame, we do not consider stars to be alive. Yet, we learned in Chapter 6 that stars "are born" when enough hydrogen collects to ignite nuclear fusion. The star then has a "life cycle" during which it changes in size as it exchanges matter and energy with its environment. At some point in its life cycle, the star may explode ("die"), ejecting matter that eventually may take form again in the birth of new stars or planets.

Thus, it is hard to define life in a simple way that includes living organisms (such as ants, trees, and humans), and that excludes crystals, stars, and dead organisms. We had similar issues in defining the words "elements" and "energy." In cases like these, definitions can cause more problems than they are worth. I prefer to explore the topic, and let our understanding develop that way. We may never reach a definition, but we will know what we are talking about.

A Systems View Of Life

To make progress in understanding life, let's focus our attention on the organisms that we all classify as living. What makes trees, ants, bacteria, and humans different from nonliving things?

What makes trees, ants, and humans different from nonliving things?

Vitalism, one of the original theories that tried to explain the nature of life, stated that living things are made of special stuff compared to nonliving things. This theory has been disproved. Living things contain the same atoms as nonliving things. In fact, organisms consist mostly of just six different atoms (carbon, hydrogen, nitrogen, oxygen, phosphorous, and sulfur). A carbon atom in any one of us is identical to a carbon atom in air, in a rock, or in baking powder. Further, in our laboratories, we can use nonliving chemicals that we keep in bottles on the shelf to make the molecules that we find in living things.

The main error in Vitalism is that this theory mistakenly states that there must be some special ingredient that either is itself alive, or that somehow changes a collection of nonliving stuff into living beings. Instead of Vitalism, we now have a systems view of life. This systems view teaches us that no single part of an organism makes it be alive rather than not alive. Instead, the system as a whole (such as a tree, an ant, or a human being) has a property called life, which its chemical parts do not individually have.

We now have a systems view of life.

LIFE

In analyzing life, we have returned to the Awesome Systems Idea that we first met in Chapter 2. Systems are made of parts, but they have properties that are qualitatively different than those of the parts ("Two Plus Two Equals Hip-Hop"). The quality of being alive is a systems property. It arises from the ways the parts work together. Life is a qualitatively different property that belongs to the system as a whole.

A single-celled organism called a paramecium.

Cells

All Earth's living things consist either of a single cell or of many cells that work together. Just as the atom can be considered the building block of Earth's matter, the cell can be considered the building block of Earth's organisms. Anything that lives on Earth today is either a single cell (such as a bacterium or an amoeba) or a multicellular organism that consists of many cells joined together.[1]

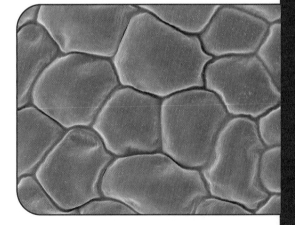

The highly magnified surface of a flower reveals that it is

Single-celled organisms are the simplest forms of life on Earth. They have parts that work together with the result that the cell is a living system. One of the most important parts is the cell membrane, a flexible wall that separates the inside of the cell from the rest of the environment.

---

[1] Viruses may be considered the exception that proves the rule. While they are not cells, they require cells in order to grow and reproduce.

Even though cells have these outer walls, they are not isolated from the environment. In order to live and grow, cells take in matter and energy, and they also release matter and energy. For example, cells take in food from their environment, and they send out waste products.

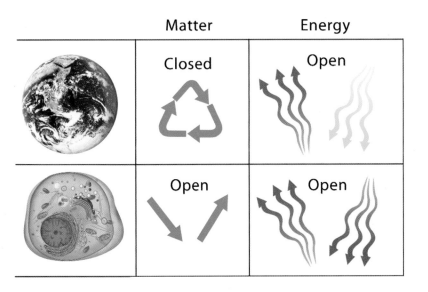

	Matter	Energy
	Closed	Open
	Open	Open

In the previous chapters, we analyzed planet Earth as a system with respect to matter, energy, and life. Unlike Earth, which is essentially a closed system for matter, cells are an open system for matter. Both Earth and cells are open systems for energy. Energy enters and leaves.

Like planet Earth, cells are also networked systems with respect to life. Cells interact with and influence each other. One of the most important ways that cells network is when they cooperate so intimately with each other that they have become part of the same organism. Plants and animals are multicellular organisms, each one consisting of a community of cells that work together.

Each of us consists of more than 200 different types of cells, and a total of about one hundred trillion cells (100,000,000,000,000). These cells work together rather than pursue their own individual agendas. One of our most frightening diseases occurs in cancer when a cell stops cooperating, and begins to multiply out of the control of the whole organism.

Cancer cells violate the multicellular cooperative agreement. They multiply in numbers, and invade

Muscle Cells

Nerve Cells

Leaf Cells

parts of the body where they do not belong. Unfortunately, this treason often results in serious disease, and even the death of the organism.

We can now answer the Who Are We question by saying, "We are Earthlings, multicellular organisms that are part of Earth's web of life." We are made of many different kinds of cells that work together. These different kinds of cells make our organs such as the heart, stomach, small intestine, pancreas, large intestine, and brain. Different organs work together in body systems, such as the circulatory system and the digestive system. The body systems combine to make a complete organism. And here we are.

Huge Molecules

I got my Ph.D. in an area of science called biochemistry. The prefix "bio" means life; biochemists investigate the molecules in living organisms. Chemists had already found that organisms have the same atoms as nonliving things. But what about the molecules that are made from those atoms?

At first, scientists thought that organisms might have special molecules that could only be made in living plants and animals. For example, the waste product urine contains a molecule called urea that occurs only in living organisms. However, in 1828, a German chemist used standard laboratory chemicals to make pure urea in his laboratory. He got so excited that he ran in the streets shouting, "Eureka! Urea! Eureka! Urea!"

From that point on, biochemists kept purifying and identifying the different kinds of molecules in bacteria, plants, and animals. They found lots of medium-sized molecules, such as sugars and amino acids. These medium-sized molecules generally consist of 10 to 50 atoms connected to each other. Urea is one of the smallest, with

eight atoms joined together (one carbon, one oxygen, two nitrogen, and four hydrogen). As with urea, biochemists could make most of these molecules fairly easily in their laboratories.

The element carbon plays a very important role in all these molecules. Carbon has a unique ability to combine with itself, forming long chains and closed structures, such as pentagons and hexagons. No other atom comes even close to carbon in this ability to form long molecules and interesting shapes. Compared to this one element, the 91 other elements are drastically limited in the ways they can combine with each other. Because of carbon's unique abilities to make long molecules with many shapes, scientists suspect that any living beings in our universe must, like us, be based on carbon.

BIG IDEA

We can make the chemicals found in living systems.

While they were having great success identifying and making the medium-sized molecules found in plants and animals, early biochemists discovered some humongous carbon-containing molecules that overwhelmed their scientific abilities. These humongous molecules had the usual six different kinds of atoms—carbon, oxygen, nitrogen, hydrogen, phosphorous, and sulfur. However, a single molecule had thousands and even millions of these atoms joined together. For many decades, biochemists were stumped in trying to understand what these molecules look like. They did not even dream of being able to make them in the laboratory.

NOW SHOWING:

CARBON

THE ELEMENT OF LIFE

STARRING

6
C
Carbon

Today we know what these humongous molecules look like, and we can make them in our laboratories. On a very practical level, our success in understanding these humongous molecules of life provides the basis for modern medicine.

In the following pages, we are going to investigate the two most important kinds of these huge molecules—proteins and DNA. After you read these pages, you may understand who you are in profoundly new ways.

Proteins

How many times have you heard about eating protein? Did you ever think why we need to eat protein?

We need proteins in our food because proteins are a very important part of our bodies. Proteins are made of building blocks called amino acids. Our bodies digest (break down) the protein in food to the level of the amino acids. Our bodies then use those amino acid building blocks to make human proteins.

What do these huge protein molecules do for us? Everything! Is this a Dr. Art Just Kidding thing? No!

Sources of protein in food.

What Proteins Do

Everything that you do, or that any other Earth organism does, is actually done at the molecular level by proteins. Specialized proteins called enzymes control and generally make possible all the chemical reactions that happen inside an organism. Different proteins are responsible for:

Actin

- digesting food (a protein called trypsin acts in our small intestine to digest proteins that we eat);
- moving from one place to another (muscles are proteins);
- burning sugars for energy (enzymes control the cell's chemical reactions, and all enzymes are proteins);
- transporting gases such as oxygen and carbon dioxide (hemoglobin in our blood is a protein);
- fighting infectious agents such as viruses (antibodies are proteins);
- acting as a chemical message that travels in the blood and helps coordinate the body's activities (a protein named insulin regulates sugar levels in the blood); and
- making accurate copies of all the molecules and structures already present in the organism (special proteins are involved in the processes whereby new proteins are made).

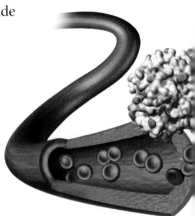

Hemoglobin

Antibody

Earth organisms rely on proteins to perform all these tasks of life. A bacterium may have 5,000 different proteins that enable it to find food, excrete waste, fight enemies, coordinate its activities, and make an exact copy of itself. A human being consists of about 40,000 different proteins that enable us to do everything that we do.

Proteins can perform all these jobs because:

- they are very large molecules
- they can fold into many different shapes
- they have different parts with different chemical properties

Each individual protein has the shape, size, and chemical abilities to superbly do just one or a few tasks. Muscle protein is great for stretching and contracting. It has absolutely no ability to carry oxygen in the blood, fight viruses, or digest starches.

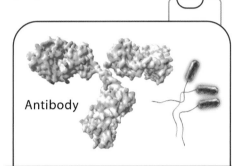

Antibody

How can proteins be so large? How can they fold into very different shapes and have so many chemical abilities? The answer is that any specific protein consists of hundreds to thousands of amino acids joined one to another in very long chains. In addition, there are 20 different amino acids with different chemical abilities and sizes.

BIG IDEA

Everything that organisms do is done by proteins.

Proteins can be very large because the chains of amino acids can be very long. Proteins are different from one another because their chain of amino acids can have very different lengths. One protein will also differ from another protein because it has different amounts of the various 20 amino acids, and because it has those amino acids in different places in its chain.

To understand proteins, it helps to visualize that each amino acid looks like a plastic bead that has a small nub at one end (its "head") and a small hole at its other end (its "tail"). The 20 different amino acids have the same heads and the same tails. They differ from each other in their "bodies."

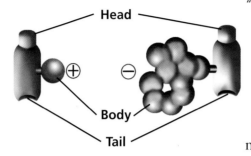

Of course, since amino acids are small molecules, they really do not have anything that looks or acts like a head, body, or tail. However, we use these words because they help illustrate how amino acids differ from each other, and how they can connect together.

Amino acids join together by having the head of one amino acid bond to the tail of another. In our bead model, the nub fits perfectly into the hole.

Notice how the sizes and electrical charges of the amino acids influence the shape of the protein chain.

Continuing in a repeating fashion, amino acids join to form a very long chain. Each amino acid connects with its head to the amino acid in front of it, and is connected by its tail to the amino acid behind it in the chain.

The "body" makes each amino acid unique. The word "body" refers to the atoms between the amino acid's head section and its tail section. These amino acid body sections have very different properties. Some of these body sections avoid contact with water; others seek contact with water; some are very small; some take up more space, and may include atoms connected together as pentagons or hexagons; some have a positive electrical charge; some have a negative electrical charge; and most have no net electrical charge.

These 20 different amino acids with their different chemical and physical properties make it possible to have a huge number of different proteins. If we connect just four amino acids to each other, there are 160,000 different combinations that we can make. There are 20 different possibilities for the first amino acid

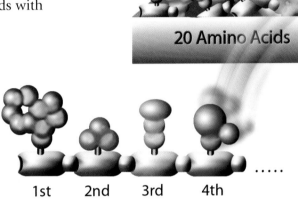

20 Amino Acids

1st   2nd   3rd   4th

There are 160,000 different combinations for just the first 4 amino acids of a protein

position, times 20 choices for the second, times 20 choices for the third, times 20 choices for the fourth amino acid position. Since proteins consist of hundreds to many thousands of amino acids linked in a chain, the possible number of different proteins is practically infinite. Because the amino acids have different sizes, chemical properties, and electrical charges, proteins have an enormous range of sizes, shapes, and chemical abilities.

Any specific protein (such as the oxygen-carrying hemoglobin in red blood cells, or the hormone insulin that regulates blood sugar levels) consists of specific amino acids joined together in a very specific order. The kinds of amino acids and their order make the protein fold into a shape that enables it to do its specific job. Removing or changing just one amino acid can drastically affect the ability of the protein to do what it normally does.

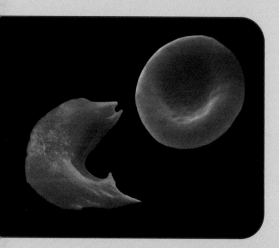

A change in just one amino acid causes sickle cell anemia.

The disease sickle cell anemia results from a change in just one amino acid out of the 177 amino acids joined together in a hemoglobin chain. Although the other 176 amino acids have exactly the same position in the chain and the same structure as in normal hemoglobin, changing that one amino acid results in red blood cells that have reduced abilities to bring oxygen to the body's cells. Changing just one amino acid in this one protein causes the person who has this kind of hemoglobin to experience episodes of pain, chronic anemia, and severe infections.

DNA

Among the many amazing things that organisms do, perhaps the most astounding is that a living organism makes copies of itself. In less than 20 minutes, a bacterium can get bigger, internally make a copy of its most essential molecules, and divide in half. Now two identical bacteria exist where previously there was just one. At this rate, one bacterium can become a million bacteria in less than seven hours.

The cells inside a multicellular organism do the same thing. That is how a single fertilized egg cell can make enough cells to become a mouse, a whale, or a human being.

A mouse embryo ten days after fertilization.

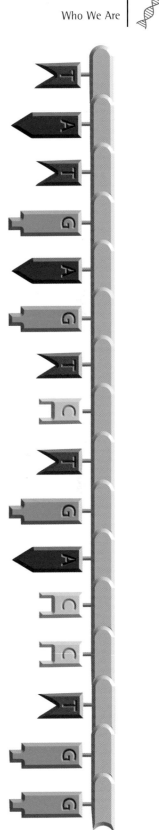

How do cells have the information that enables them to know how to become a bacterium, or a mouse nose cell, or a human brain cell? How do they copy that information so each new cell knows how to do its job, including reproducing itself?

By the 1950s, scientists had proved that humongous molecules known as nucleic acids play the main role in storing information and in passing the information to future generations. In this book, we will focus on a kind of nucleic acid called DNA.

Similar to proteins, nucleic acids also consist of smaller pieces that join head-to-tail in long chains. In the case of nucleic acids, the smaller pieces are called nucleotide bases, or just bases for short. DNA consists of four bases (called A, T, G, and C). It helps to picture each base as having a head, tail, and body.

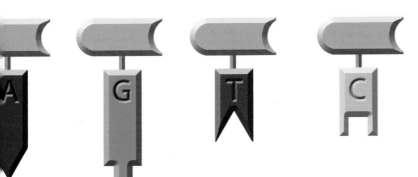

The heads of the four DNA bases are all the same, and the tails of the four DNA bases are all the same. The "body" section makes the four bases different from each other. Notice the illustration along the side of this page showing how the bases connect with each other. They form a long chain with the "body" of each base, sticking out in a perpendicular direction.

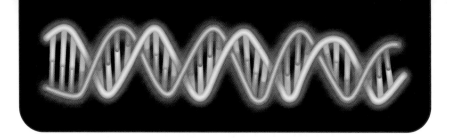

A DNA molecule consists of two chains that wind around each other in a double helix. Wherever there is an A on one chain, it loosely pairs with a T on the opposite chain. Similarly, T always pairs with A, G pairs with C, and C pairs with G.

Let's see how a DNA molecule can get copied. The illustration on the next page shows a DNA molecule as two vertical chains, next to each other. This way of showing them next to each other makes it easier to see how DNA gets copied. Note again that A and T are always opposite each other. The same holds true for G and C.

The connections vertically up and down each chain are very strong. The horizontal base pairs across the two chains are much weaker. As a result, the chains can separate from each other relatively easily.

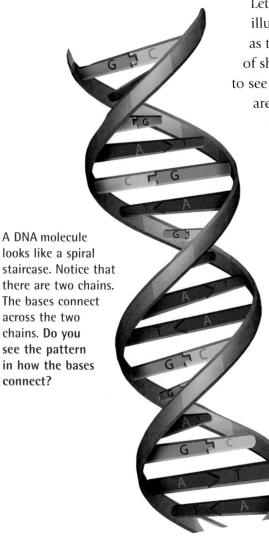

A DNA molecule looks like a spiral staircase. Notice that there are two chains. The bases connect across the two chains. **Do you see the pattern in how the bases connect?**

As the chains separate, the cell can form a new companion chain along each of the separated chains. The growth of the companion chain uses the same base pairing rules (A with T; T with A; G with C; and C with G). When the cell is finished, it will have two double-chain DNA molecules that are identical to the original starting double-chain DNA molecule. The cell can then split in half, with each of the two new cells getting its own copy of the same DNA as was in the original cell.

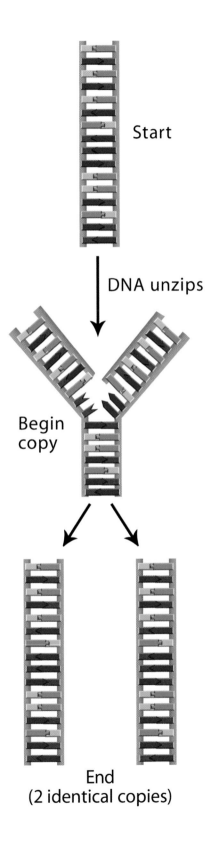

Start

DNA unzips

Begin copy

**End
(2 identical copies)**

Thus, the structure of DNA and its base pairing rules show how DNA can be readily copied. A father's sperm cell brings its DNA molecules to join the DNA molecules in a mother's egg cell. The resulting single fertilized egg cell has a set of DNA molecules from both the mother and the father. It then grows and divides forming a human being with trillions of cells. Each of these cells has its own copy of the set of DNA molecules contributed by the mother and father in the original fertilized egg cell.

BIG IDEA

The structure of DNA explains how it can be copied.

This copying makes it possible for children to have DNA that has the same order of bases as the DNA in their parents. However, we still have a huge question. How does a DNA molecule work? What is so special about the order of the bases in a DNA molecule? How does that molecule provide the information to make a human being instead of a mouse, fruit fly, or sunflower?

Earth Life Is Bilingual And Has A Code

How does DNA have the information so that a daughter looks like her mother?

Earlier in this chapter, we learned that proteins do everything that you or any other Earth organism does. The proteins generally make possible all the chemical reactions that happen inside organisms. They also help form many of the organism's structures. Therefore, if some program told the cells of an organism how to make each of its proteins, then the organism would have the information that it needs. The program tells the cells how to make their specific proteins, and the proteins then do everything else. The nucleic acids are that program.

Once we discovered the structure of DNA, the next step in the detective mystery involved figuring out the code that enables DNA to tell cells how to make specific proteins. Any given protein consists of a chain of amino acids that are linked together in a specific order. To make a specific protein, the cell needs instructions telling it which amino acid to start with, which amino acid to put in the second position, which amino acid to put in the third position, continuing all the way to the last amino acid in the protein chain.

Somehow the DNA has the information to place the correct amino acid in the right position for each protein.

An interesting way to think about this task is to consider proteins to be a kind of language that has 20 different letters. Each letter represents a different amino acid. Any specific protein is like a page of text with one letter following the other spelling out the very long protein "word."

We can think of DNA as being a different language that consists of only four letters (A, T, G, and C). Somehow, the DNA language can specify the order of letters in the protein language. In other words, the order of the bases in a section of DNA is a code that somehow corresponds to the order of amino acids in a specific protein.

What kind of code can it be? Can it be a one-letter code? The base A could represent one amino acid; T could code for a second amino acid; G could code for a third: and C could code for a fourth. With a one-letter DNA code, cells could make proteins that had only four different amino acids. But proteins contain twenty different amino acids.

How about a two-letter DNA code? As you can see, there are sixteen different two-letter combinations of the four DNA bases. A two-letter DNA code almost works. However, for life, almost is not good enough.

AA AT AG AC
TA TT TG TC
CA CT CG CC
GA GT GG GC

In contrast, a 3-letter DNA code has 64 combinations (you do the math!). This is more than enough for the 20 amino acids, and also for punctuation marks such as "start here" and "stop here." And guess what? Life uses a 3-letter DNA code, which is called the genetic code.

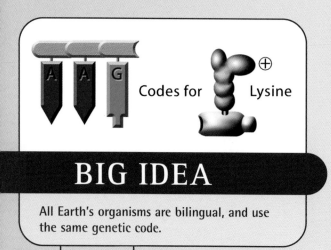

Codes for ⊕ Lysine

BIG IDEA

All Earth's organisms are bilingual, and use the same genetic code.

How does that code work? The cell "reads" a sequence of DNA bases in 3-letter chunks. Each of the 3-letter combinations indicates to the cell which amino acid to use as it makes a specific protein. For example, the 3-letter combination AAG indicates the amino acid lysine.[2]

All Earth life uses the same genetic code. The 3-letter combination AAG corresponds to the amino acid lysine for bacteria, fruit flies, redwood trees, mushrooms, jellyfish, and humans. Scientists can take the genetic instructions for making a human protein, and put this human DNA into a mouse, fruit fly, or a bacterium. That organism can then make the identical human protein. At the molecular level, we are incredibly related.

Earlier in this chapter, we discussed the disease sickle cell anemia where a change in one amino acid in the hemoglobin protein causes this serious disease. Generally, the cause of this disease is a change in a single letter in the stretch of about 500 DNA bases that code for the hemoglobin protein.

Normal hemoglobin DNA sequence for the 3rd through 9th amino acid positions:

... ... CTG ACT CCT GAG GAG AAG TCT ... ...

Sickle cell DNA sequence for the 3rd through 9th amino acid positions:

... ... CTG ACT CCT GTG GAG AAG TCT ... ...

"T" replaces "A" in the code for the 6th amino acid (changing the 3-letter sequence from GAG to GTG). The result is a change from an amino acid that has a negative charge and that likes water to an amino acid that has no electrical charge and that avoids water. Thus,

[2] Since there are more 3-letter combinations than there are amino acids, most amino acids actually have more than one 3-letter combination that specify that amino acid. For example, the triplets AAA and AAG both code for the amino acid lysine. Some 3-letter combinations mean "start here" or "stop here."

the change in one base causes a change in just one amino acid. As a result, the altered hemoglobin protein folds into a different shape. Red blood cells with the altered hemoglobin develop an unusual sickle shape, do not carry oxygen well, and the person suffers from a serious disease.

The Table below compares proteins and DNA, summarizing how they are different and how they are related.

Comparing Proteins and DNA		
FEATURE	PROTEIN	DNA
What it does in a cell	Does everything that a cell needs to do, and makes up some of the cell structures.	Stores and transfers information; tells the cell what to do and how to do it.
Building blocks	20 different amino acids	4 different nucleotide bases
What a chain is made out of	Amino acids linked head to tail	Nucleotide bases linked head to tail
Number of chains	A protein can have one or more chains that can have tight or weak connections across the chains.	Each DNA molecule consists of two long chains in a double helix, with weak base pair connections across the two chains.
How it does what it does	Each protein folds into a specific 3-dimensional shape based on the order of the amino acids in its chain. That shape and the chemical properties of its amino acids enable it to do what it does.	All DNA molecules have generally the same shape. The order of the DNA bases specifies the order of amino acids in a protein chain. A sequence of 3 nucleic acid "letters" codes for a particular amino acid.

This chapter has provided a simplified, but fairly accurate, description of how multicellular organisms work at the level of our molecules. My only concern is that you may have the impression that DNA is the "boss" of the organism. Cells are systems, and there is no "master molecule." The molecules inside the cell all influence each other.

In the next chapter, we are going to explore how life and the environment have changed over time. This exploration will add more dimensions to understanding who we are.

STOP & THINK

This chapter has lots of illustrations. I needed them to explain what proteins and DNA look like, and how they do their jobs.

Skillful readers use illustrations in lots of ways. As they start a chapter, they may skim ahead, and look at the photos and drawings. They start to get an idea of what is in the chapter. They may think about, or even write down, what they already know about the topic, and what they think they might learn.

Here's a reading strategy you can use while you read a chapter. As you read a page, interact with its illustrations. Try to figure out what each one means, and why the author drew it exactly that way, with all the details.

Just as it can help to explain a new idea in your own words, you can make your own drawing to explain what you think are the main ideas on a page. If you are reading with others, share your drawings, and compare their strengths and weaknesses in portraying those main ideas.

You can also use illustrations to review after you finish a chapter. Look at each illustration and write a sentence or two highlighting its most important information. For example, the top illustration on page 170 shows how amino acids are similar to each other by having the same heads and tails, and that they are different in their bodies. The drawing on the bottom of that page shows . . .

By now, you may have noticed a Big Idea in reading strategies. They usually involve helping you become aware of your own thinking processes. Observe yourself like a scientist who notices and says, "Whoops! I did not understand those words I just read. I was just pronouncing them to myself while I was thinking about dinner. Better read them again."

With illustrations, your inner, self-observing scientist might say, "I understand the illustration on page 176 showing how the DNA code helps to select which amino acid to put in each position of the protein chain. I can draw that better than what's in the book. Check this out, Dr. Art!"

www.guidetoscience.net

THE FAMOUS E WORD

Chapter 11 –
The Famous E Word

What I Know About Evolution

Back in Chapter 6, we explored how the universe has changed over time. In its early years, the only elements were hydrogen and helium, and these two gases were spread evenly throughout space. Neither stars nor galaxies existed. Today, our universe has more than 90 elements, and billions of stars and galaxies. Gravity caused the hydrogen gas to gather into stars. Nuclear fusion explains how these stars then produced all the bigger elements.

Similarly, our planet has changed over time. Earth began with molecules much simpler than those that occur here today. It began with small molecules such as water, carbon dioxide, methane, and ammonia. Today, our planet includes humongous molecules such as proteins and DNA. Even more impressive, these molecules are part of awesome creatures that we call bacteria, fruit flies, redwood trees, turtles, and human beings.

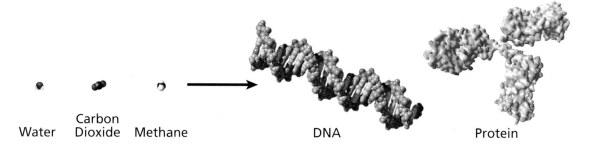

| Water | Carbon Dioxide | Methane | | DNA | | Protein |

Scientists use the word **evolution** when they describe these kinds of changes. Both the universe and life evolve. Nuclear fusion in stars explains how the universe has complex atoms even though it started with just hydrogen and helium. Similarly, the processes of biological evolution explain how Earth has complex organisms even though life started with much simpler, single-celled organisms.

182

Many people have difficulty accepting that Earth's organisms are here as a result of biological evolution. Even people who recognize the reality of biological evolution often have wrong ideas about it. In this and the next chapter, we will explore evolution to better understand how it operates, and what lessons we can learn from it.

What does evolution mean to you? Before reading further in this chapter, please take some time to write answers to the following questions.

What do you know about evolution?

What opinions do you have about evolution?

What do you think this chapter will tell you about evolution?

Meat Eating Caterpillars In Hawaii

How did life reach its present condition? Evolution explains the history of life on Earth. It teaches how the millions of different species could arise, and how organisms possess the amazing features that enable them to prosper.

Human societies have become separated from the world of nature.

One reason that people do not understand evolution is because human societies have become so separated from the world of nature. We experience primarily a world of houses, cars, offices, trains, supermarkets, electric lights, parking lots, and televisions. We buy our food packaged in plastic. We interact with machines, other humans, and a few kinds of pets and pests.

Why does Earth have so many different organisms? Why do they exist only in specific locations? People who live close to nature confront the incredible diversity and astounding adaptability of life.

If you want to experience the wonders of the natural world, leave the cities and travel to wild areas in Hawaii. The Hawaiian Islands are one of the best places to encounter the natural world, and to experience life's enormous diversity. On these isolated islands, scientists find organisms that do not exist anywhere else. These include crickets that do not see, caterpillars that catch flies, and more than 600 different species of fruit flies (the world total is only about 1,500).

FREE 1 TICKET TO HAWAII ON ANY AIRLINE (AS LONG AS YOU PROMISE TO STUDY BIODIVERSITY WHILE YOU ARE THERE)

Take the case of the caterpillars, also known as inchworms. In practically every other location on our planet, caterpillars only eat plants. In contrast, at least 18 species of meat-eating caterpillars live in Hawaii. Dr. Steven Lee Montgomery described how he discovered the first of these species:

"When I spotted the inchworm eating a fly as large as itself, I was incredulous. How could a sluggish caterpillar manage to snag a fly? What sort of insect version of a movie monster was this? I thought all inchworms were vegetarians. I captured the caterpillar, climbed out of the volcanic cone on the island of Hawaii, and returned to my lab at the University of Hawaii in Honolulu. There, I expected, my find would revert to normal plant-eating behavior. Two days later a leaf in the bottle remained untouched, so I slipped in a fly. It landed near the inchworm. The inchworm raised itself slightly. The fly stepped closer, brushing the inchworm. Suddenly the inchworm swung sideways, snatched the fly in its talons and devoured it, leaving a few wings and leg tips, like clean-picked bones on a plate."[1]

Wouldn't hurt a fly?

---

[1] Steven L. Montgomery, The Case of the Killer Caterpillars, National Geographic, August, 1983, pages 219-225.
One percent of caterpillar species outside Hawaii eat slow, crawling, soft-bodied insects.

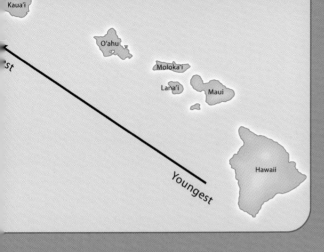

Kaua'i
O'ahu
Moloka'i
Lana'i Maui
'st
Youngest
Hawaii

Evolution explains why and how Hawaii has so many examples of organisms that live nowhere else on our planet. Each of the Hawaiian islands started as a volcano, slowly growing from the bottom of the ocean. Beginning with red-hot lava, these new islands emerged thousands of miles from any continent, and started without living organisms.

With time, each island cooled and slowly became a great place for life. Any species of organism that landed on a bare island had the opportunity to evolve in new and fascinating ways. New ways of life were available; predator enemies from the mainland were absent. If you are crickets living in a cave, you do not need to see. If you are the first fruit flies, then your species can evolve to live on new kinds of food and in ways that were taken by other fly species back home on the continents. And even caterpillars can evolve to catch and eat flies.

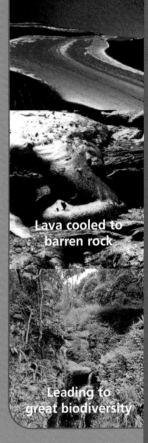

Started with lava

Lava cooled to barren rock

Leading to great biodiversity

What Dead Bodies Tell Us

Not only does evolution explain the current distribution of plants and animals, it also explains why and where we find fossils. Today we know that 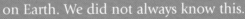fossils are the remains of organisms that used to live on Earth. We did not always know this.

The earliest fossils found by naturalists were mostly of small organisms. They had been viewed as either slightly changed examples of known species, or as species that still existed in unexplored regions. However, this idea changed as humans discovered large skeletons.

Trilobite fossil

Mammoths provided the first firm clues to Western civilization that fossils represent species that had once existed, but have now disappeared from Earth. When mammoth carcasses were discovered buried in snow, we knew without a doubt that different animals used to live on our planet. When dinosaur fossils were discovered, we realized that reptiles once dominated life on our planet.

To better understand fossils, let's imagine that cities die, and get replaced every 20 years. The new city is built on top of the old one, and when it dies, a new city is constructed on top of it. Imagine that you could take a vertical slice through the cities, and examine from the oldest city on the bottom up to the newest city on top.

The bottom city has absolutely no electronic communication or entertainment machines. As you can see, the second oldest city and all the cities above it have telephones. Check out which cities have cell phones, radios, home computers, and televisions. Based on what you see, list the order in which these devices were invented from oldest to most recent.

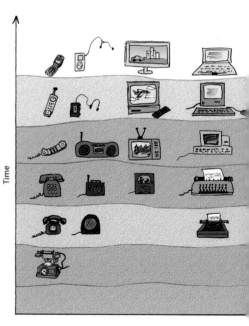

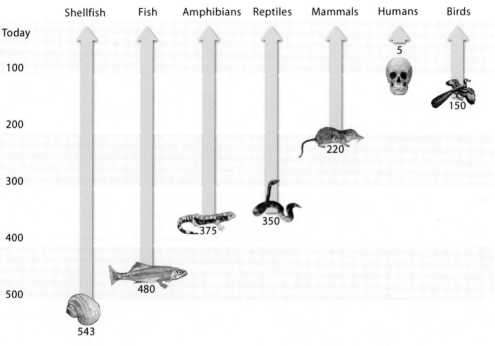

Shellfish Fish Amphibians Reptiles Mammals Humans Birds

Today

100

200

300

400

500

600

5

150

220

350

375

480

543

Fossils provide this kind of evidence for scientists who study life's history on Earth. When a river erodes rock to form a canyon, the walls of the canyon display different kinds of fossils at different heights. Generally, the oldest rocks are at the bottom of the canyon, with the youngest rocks at the top.

By examining the different fossils at different heights, scientists can trace how life has changed over hundreds of millions of years. Examine the illustration above to see when fossils of different kinds of organisms first appear in the fossil record. The vertical dimension of this figure represents millions of years ago. For example, fossils of birds first appear about 150 million years ago. Older rocks do not contain bird fossils. Therefore, we know that birds first appeared on our planet around 150 million years ago, a long time after fish, reptiles, and mammals.

BIG IDEA

Evolution explains who used to live when, and who lives where now.

A Tree Of Life

We can illustrate the history of life on our planet as a "Tree of Life." The bottom parts of the tree represent the early stages of life billions of years ago. Going up the tree takes us closer to the present.

Today's organisms are on the outermost edges of the tree. The roots and base of the tree represent the first single-celled organisms. All Earth life today shares these microscopic organisms as very distant ancestors.

The right side of the drawing features vertebrates, animals that have a backbone. Note that this illustration is biased in favor of vertebrates. Animals with backbones account for less than 5% of the planet's known species.

At point A, approximately 500 million years ago (mya), the first animals with backbones inhabited our planet, leading eventually to all of today's fish, reptiles, amphibians, birds, and mammals. These vertebrates were ocean fish. Reptiles, vertebrates that could spend their entire lives on land, first appeared about 280 mya.

Mammals first appeared at Point B, about 210 mya. All of today's mammals and reptiles share a most recent common ancestor at point B. Since that time, reptiles and mammals have been evolving. Today's snakes are as

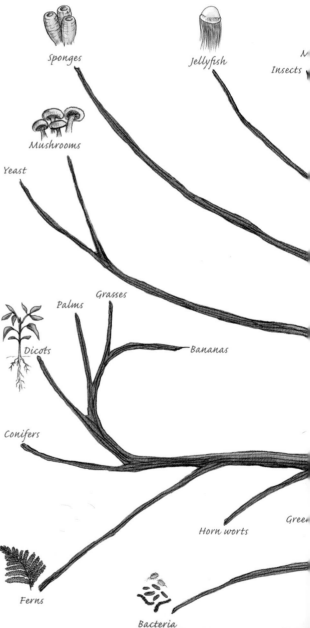

Sponges

Jellyfish

Insects

Mushrooms

Yeast

Grasses

Palms

Dicots

Bananas

Conifers

Horn worts

Gree

Ferns

Bacteria

distant in time from the common ancestor at point B as are mice, pigeons, and humans.

Birds and reptiles last shared a common ancestor at point C. In comparison, the most recent common ancestor for birds and mammals lived further back in time at point B. Therefore, birds are more closely related to reptiles than they are to mammals.

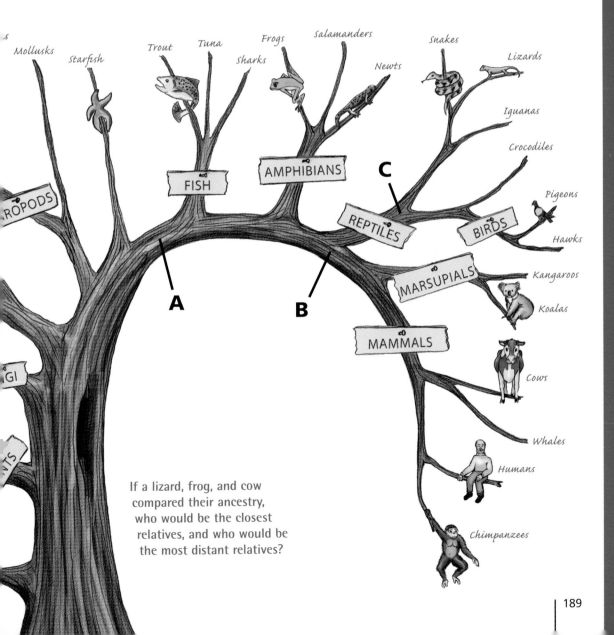

If a lizard, frog, and cow compared their ancestry, who would be the closest relatives, and who would be the most distant relatives?

What Live Bodies Tell Us

Not only does evolution explain who lives where today and how they are related, it also explains the weird features of different bodies. You might wonder what kinds of body features need to be explained. Here are some examples.

Some snakes have bones generally associated with walking. Only female bees have a stinger. Some blind animal species have eyes, including lens and retina, that are totally covered by skin. A human embryo starts to form a tail, and, on rare occasions, a baby is born with an external tail.

Why does this snake have a pelvis and leg bones?

Some snakes, such as the python and boa constrictor, have a simple pelvis and back legs. These bones are completely hidden within the body. Since pythons and boa constrictors do not walk, they do not use these bones. Evolution explains that these bones are a part of these snakes' ancestral history. Pythons and boa constrictors evolved from four-legged reptiles that used a pelvis and legs to walk on land.

Why don't male bees have a stinger? Hives would benefit from having male defenders that could sting. It turns out that the stinger evolved from the part of the female bee's body that lays eggs, depositing each egg in a honeycomb. In these social insects, the queen bee became the only female who lays eggs. The egg-laying body part on all the other females lost that function. Over time, that body part evolved into a sharp-pointed stinger. Since male bees never had this egg-laying body part, they do not have a stinger.

Magnified bee stinger

As a fertilized human egg grows inside the mother, the developing embryo has many features that provide evidence of our ancestry. For example, when the embryo is about five weeks old, a beginning tail accounts for about 10% of its entire length. This structure includes beginning bones, spinal cord, and nerves, all properly arranged. However, as the embryo continues to develop, cells in this tail die, the immune system gets rid of the cells, and a normal baby does not have an external tail. Instead, we have a small, internal tailbone called the coccyx.

Very rarely, a baby is born with an external tail. About 30% of the reported cases are not true tails. However, the other 70% are true tails, which, on newborn babies, can be as long as 5 inches. The true tail can move and contract. It has normal skin, and includes nerves, blood vessels, and muscles. Because of our evolutionary ancestry, we all have the DNA information to make an external tail. Newer DNA programming stops the growth of the tail, and almost all humans enter the world without an external tail.

In addition to explaining weird body parts, evolution explains why the standard body parts are made the way they are. The *Encyclopedia Britannica* article on evolution states it this way:

> "The skeletons of turtles, horses, humans, birds, and bats are strikingly similar, in spite of the different ways of life of these animals and the diversity of their environments. The correspondence, bone by bone, can be easily seen in the limbs, but also in every other part of the body. From a purely practical point of view, it is incomprehensible that a turtle should swim, a horse run, a person write, and a bird or bat fly with structures built of the same bones. An engineer could design better limbs in each case. But if it is accepted that all of these skeletons inherited their structures from a common ancestor and became modified only as they adapted to different ways of life, the similarity of their structures makes sense."[2]

2 Reprinted with permission from *Encyclopædia Britannica*, ©2005 by Encyclopædia Britannica, Inc.

Turtle

Horse

Human

Bird

Bat

In other words, all these animals have a common ancestor that had four limbs that were made of bones. In turtles, these bones changed over time to maximize swimming abilities. In horses, they changed over time to maximize running abilities. In birds, the same bones changed over time to maximize flying abilities. In humans, the same bones have changed over time so we can make and use tools such as spears, pots, and pencils. When we look at those bones today, we see evidence that life developed over millions of years, and that today's different species have common ancestors.

What Molecules Tell Us

In the previous chapter, we learned about proteins and DNA. All Earth organisms use proteins to do what they do, and nucleic acids to store the information. We also learned about the genetic code that translates from DNA to proteins. All life on Earth uses essentially the same genetic code. This unity of life is exactly what we would expect based on evolution teaching that we all share a common ancestor. The first single-celled organisms evolved the genetic code, and all life since then has used it.

We can use these big molecules to do experiments to test evolution. Scientists developed the Tree of Life mostly by examining fossils and today's body structures. Once they learned how to analyze proteins and DNA, they investigated to compare those molecules in different organisms. They then compared what they learned from the molecules with what they had previously learned from fossils and bones. If evolution is correct, then human proteins and DNA should resemble mouse proteins and DNA more than the same molecules in a fruit fly or a sunflower.

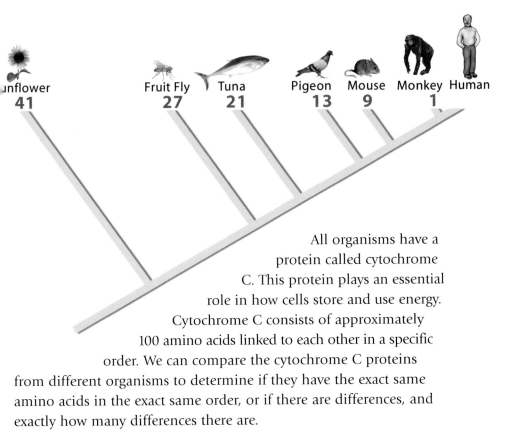

unflower	Fruit Fly	Tuna	Pigeon	Mouse	Monkey	Human
41	**27**	**21**	**13**	**9**	**1**	

All organisms have a protein called cytochrome C. This protein plays an essential role in how cells store and use energy. Cytochrome C consists of approximately 100 amino acids linked to each other in a specific order. We can compare the cytochrome C proteins from different organisms to determine if they have the exact same amino acids in the exact same order, or if there are differences, and exactly how many differences there are.

The diagram above includes the results of comparing human cytochrome C with the cytochrome C from six organisms. For example, this protein in monkeys is the same as human cytochrome C except for a change in one amino acid (number of amino acid differences is shown in red). The same protein in sunflowers has 41 changes compared with the human cytochrome C. The less related the organism is to humans, the more differences there are in the cytochrome C.

These measurements have been made for many different organisms using both DNA and protein. Organisms that have more recent common ancestors resemble each other more on the DNA and protein levels than organisms that are less closely related. Analysis of these molecules provides essentially the same history of life as had been patiently constructed by comparing fossils and body structures. The evidence from molecules strongly confirms an evolutionary tree of life.

How Does Evolution Happen?

How could life on Earth evolve from simpler organisms and result in an amazing diversity of complex organisms? Charles Darwin, the man whose name is most closely associated with solving this puzzle, hesitated for many years before he publicly announced his answer in 1858. He knew that the idea of evolution would create controversy.

Darwin proposed two related ideas. First, he stated that life evolves with species changing over time. In other words, today's species result from a long historical change process reaching back to the first organisms. All species are related, and can be traced back to a common ancestor many, many millions of years ago.

Darwin's second proposal stated how evolution occurs. This idea has become generally known as **natural selection**. According to natural selection, organisms that have features that improve their ability to live and reproduce in a given environment will tend to increase in numbers. Many different kinds of features can provide these advantages. Examples include features that help obtain food, avoid enemies, resist disease, attract mates, and produce offspring.

Examples of natural selection in action:
A stick insect blending into its environment (Do you see it?)
A cheetah running to catch an antelope
A sunflower turning its leaves to catch more sunlight
A peacock displaying its feathers to attract a mate
A tribe cooperating to hunt buffalo
A peach tree packaging its seeds in sweet fruit

Cheetahs that can run faster will generally have better chances of living and reproducing. A male peacock whose feathers attract more females will have way more descendants than a male who does not attract females. An apple tree that attracts more animals to eat its fruit is more likely to have its seeds brought to new locations where they can grow into new trees.

We can readily observe natural selection. For example, we currently have problems with harmful bacteria that now resist many antibiotics. By producing large amounts of these antibiotics and using them foolishly, humans have created conditions that select for disease organisms that resist antibiotics. In the presence of antibiotics, a tuberculosis bacterium that resists the antibiotic has a much greater ability to survive and reproduce than a tuberculosis bacterium that is sensitive to the antibiotic. As a result of this natural selection, our world today has a much higher percentage of disease-causing bacteria that resist many antibiotics.

Natural selection can also be readily observed in situations that do not involve humans. For example, the American Southwest has many populations of sandy-colored, rock pocket mice. These rodents blend well with their natural background as they hunt for food. Their color helps protect them from predators.

In a few locations, the natural background color is darker because of lava flows from ancient times. In these areas, the rock pocket mice have dark coats instead of sandy coats. Taking advantage of the same camouflage strategy, natural selection has resulted in populations of dark-colored mice in one kind of location and sandy-colored mice everywhere else.

Darwin's proposal of natural selection as the mechanism for evolution actually involves four conditions

1

Individuals in a population of organisms vary in characteristics that are inherited.

2

Organisms produce more offspring than the environment can support

3

Individuals compete for survival and reproductive success.

4

Organisms whose variations increase their ability to survive and reproduce in the current environment are most likely to pass those variations to their descendants.

So far we have focused on the third and fourth conditions. We discussed organisms competing, and the features that increase the chances of having descendants. We assumed that the environment cannot support all the organisms that are produced (condition 2). This situation occurs all the time. Organisms typically produce many more offspring than can survive. Think about rabbits. If all rabbit babies lived and reproduced, the planet would be covered with rabbits.

Natural selection also assumes the first condition, that individuals in a population are different from each other, and that these differences are inherited. Without these variations, all members of a population would be identical. All individuals would have the same chance of succeeding and reproducing. There would be no natural selection, and no evolution.

Natural selection also depends on these differences being inherited. If differences existed, but were not inherited, evolution by natural selection would not happen. Without this inheritance, the kittens of a fast cheetah would not be any faster than the kittens of a slow cheetah. An increase in speed could not be selected and improved from generation to generation.

Darwin did not know how life passes information from one generation to the next. He also did not know how characteristics could vary, and how inheritance works. Today's scientists know, and so will you after you read the next section.

Changes That Are Inherited

Just looking at people shows us that individuals in a population vary in their characteristics. Anything changes that can possibly change. We have different height, skin (color, oiliness, marks), artistic ability, hair (color, type, amount), health, emotional sensitivity, etc.

The key point with respect to natural selection and evolution is that these variations occur randomly. If it is at all possible for a characteristic to vary, it will. And it will vary in as many ways as the body's DNA and proteins make possible. As a result, any population of sexually reproducing organisms will consist of individuals that vary in some way from every other individual in the population (excepting identical twins).

Many variations are always present. Each individual in a population of organisms differs from the average in many ways. When the environment favors a particular variation, this characteristic can, over time, become a prominent feature of that population.

Normal DNA

DNA with specific change in one DNA base

What causes these changes? You know that the DNA codes instructions for making proteins. If the DNA changes, then the proteins may change. If the proteins change, the characteristics of the whole organism may change. In other words, differences in DNA from one organism to another cause changes in the characteristics of those organisms. The changes could be related to a wide variety of characteristics. such as height, color, intelligence, allergies, or blood type.

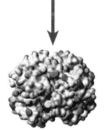

Normal hemoglobin

Changed hemoglobin

HEALTHY
Healthy person

SICK

Person with sickle cell anemia

But what makes the DNA change? The DNA in cells is constantly exposed to chemicals and electromagnetic radiation that can cause changes in its bases (remember that four bases are the letters of the DNA language). In addition, mistakes happen.

Errors occur when the DNA gets copied. Each human cell has DNA that consists of six billion bases in specific order on each of the two strands. Copying that DNA occurs over several hours at the rate of 500,000 bases per second. During this hectic copying, errors occur such as putting one or more bases in the wrong location, or even losing or adding sections of the DNA.

These changes to the DNA sequence of bases are called **mutations**. Changes in the DNA can cause changes to proteins, which can cause changes in the organism's characteristics. These changes are inherited because they happen to the cell's information system, its DNA.

Changing one of more bases in the DNA can cause changes in that organism's proteins. As a result, that individual may have different characteristics than other members of the same population. The vast majority of mutations are harmful or neutral, and therefore are not selected. However, very occasionally a mutation helps an organism survive and reproduce. In that case, its children will have the same changes in their DNA. They will inherit the altered DNA, and will therefore make the changed protein that will help them succeed in that environment.

BIG IDEA

Life has diversity built into its very core.

Biology teaches that life naturally generates an abundance of variations that can be inherited. Life has diversity built into its very core. Charles Darwin did not know how life generates this enormous diversity. Now you do. If you can figure out how to travel in time, go back and tell him.

Selecting Random Changes

The changes in the DNA provide the pool of possible variations in characteristics; the environment determines the direction of evolution. For example, the changes in DNA may enable a cricket to have better vision, or the changes may reduce its vision. The environment selects the "better vision changes" for crickets living in the meadow, and the "don't waste energy on vision changes" for the Hawaii crickets living exclusively in caves. Evolution takes advantage of random changes in the DNA to select those changes that help the organism survive and reproduce in the current environment.

It is relatively easy to understand that on dark rocks, dark mice will have a better chance of surviving than light colored mice. Similarly, it makes sense that in the presence of an antibiotic, bacteria that resist the drug will replace those that are killed by the antibiotic. Scientists can show that a change in just one or two proteins can change a mouse's color or a bacterium's sensitivity to an antibiotic. These simple changes are then selected depending on the environment.

What about more complicated characteristics such as speed, hunting ability, vision, or intelligence? Scientists know that these characteristics result from many proteins working together. In these cases, evolution proceeds through many small, step-by-step changes.

A variation that improves an organism's ability to survive by a tiny amount, say 1%, will become widely distributed in the population in a relatively short time. We would not notice a 1% improvement even in our own lives, but evolution can readily track and encourage such small changes.

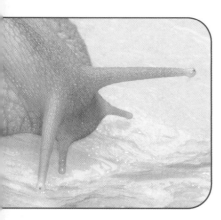

Primitive eyes of snail

Consider a herd of deer that live in a forest that can support 100 deer. A mutation occurs that increases speed, and provides a 1% advantage in surviving and reproducing. In less than 300 years, all the deer will have that mutation. That may seem like a long time to us, but it is less than a blink in Earth's history.

People who have problems accepting evolution often say that natural selection cannot produce complicated adaptations such as the ability to see or fly. Actually, scientists provide very reasonable explanations for the evolution of these features.

Consider vision. Any creature that could dimly sense light would have an immense advantage over its totally blind relatives and neighbors. Even slight improvements would progressively be selected, leading to better and better vision.

Highly developed human eye

Because they provide such great survival advantages, eyes have independently evolved many times. The illustration below shows the kinds of relatively small steps that can lead from blindness to clear vision. It was inspired by the detailed analysis provided by Richard Dawkins in Chapter 5 of his book, *Climbing Mount Improbable* (W.W. Norton & Company, 1996).

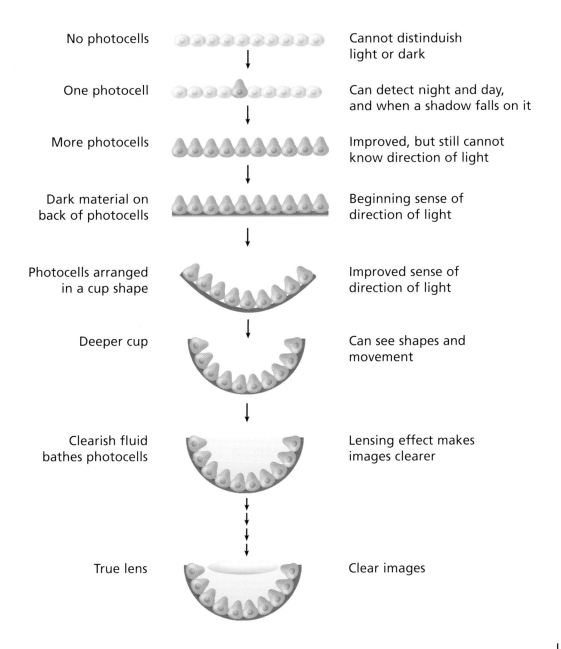

No photocells	Cannot distinduish light or dark
One photocell	Can detect night and day, and when a shadow falls on it
More photocells	Improved, but still cannot know direction of light
Dark material on back of photocells	Beginning sense of direction of light
Photocells arranged in a cup shape	Improved sense of direction of light
Deeper cup	Can see shapes and movement
Clearish fluid bathes photocells	Lensing effect makes images clearer
True lens	Clear images

Some people think that the randomness of the variations poses a problem for evolution. If changes occur randomly, how can something as complex as an eye come into existence? The answer is that while the changes are random, natural selection is not random. Natural selection always moves populations of organisms toward surviving better in their environment. If the environment consistently favors organisms that can see well, then natural selection will steadily lead to better vision. If the environment consistently favors organisms that do not waste energy on sight, then natural selection will steadily lead to blindness.

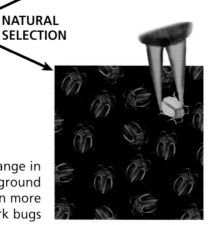

Change in background results in more light bugs

Grey background; Equal numbers of light and dark colored bugs.

NATURAL SELECTION

Change in background results in more dark bugs

It is easy to make the mistake of thinking that organisms have these variations because they are trying to fit better in the environment. On the contrary, the changes occur randomly, without design or purpose. Bacteria do not encounter antibiotics, and then decide how to become resistant. Insects do not notice that the environment has become darker, and then try to have a darker color. Crickets living in caves do not decide to become blind.

Instead, in populations of organisms, there are always variations: such as giraffes with different size necks, and insects with different shades of color. Random variations provide the raw materials that natural selection can build upon. Depending on the environment, different variations will be selected, resulting in populations that are better adapted to their current environment.

This chapter has introduced us to the **Awesome Evolution Idea**. In brief, all organisms today share common ancestors. The species inhabiting Earth have changed enormously over time, and natural selection plays an important role in causing those changes.

In the next chapter, we will explore what happened to a group of organisms that dominated Earth for millions of years. Their characteristics enabled them to prosper and reproduce in many different kinds of environments on all Earth's continents except Antarctica. But those environments changed in one fell swoop on December 26th at midnight.

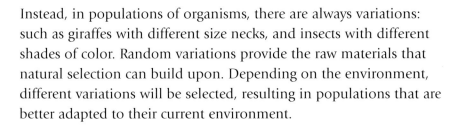

Awesome Idea

EVOLUTION
All organisms today share common ancestors. The species inhabiting Earth have changed enormously over time, and natural selection plays an important role in causing biological evolution.

STOP & THINK

Early in this chapter, I asked you to write your answers to three questions:

What do you know about evolution?

What opinions do you have about evolution?

What do you think Dr. Art is going to tell you about evolution?

Look at what you wrote. Compare what you knew then with what you know now. Do you still have the same opinions? Did I tell you what you thought I was going to tell you?

The next chapter will take us even deeper into evolution and the history of life on our planet. Please fill out the chart below. We will return to it at the end of the next chapter. If you want to write more about any of the statements, go for it. Writing helps you know what you are thinking, and even gives you new ideas. I often surprise myself when I see what I have written, and that is one reason why I like to write.

EVOLUTION STATEMENT	AGREE	DISAGREE	NOT SURE
Evolution explains how plants and animals developed on Earth.			
I personally do not think that humans evolved from simpler life forms.			
Because of evolution, organisms keep becoming better and better.			
Evolution teaches that God does not exist.			
I understand how long a billion years is.			
The development of human beings was the purpose of evolution.			
The science that enables me to drive a car, get a flu shot, or use a computer is very different from the science that teaches evolution.			

www.guidetoscience.net

MIDNIGHT DECEMBER 26

Beginning of Earth

History Of Life On Earth

Earth formed four billion five hundred and fifty million (4,550,000,000) years ago. Later in this chapter, I will explain how scientists figure out the age of things like rocks, fossils, and planets.

During those millions of years, life on Earth changed in many ways. We can illustrate these changes by compressing all of Earth's history into a time scale of one year. When we treat all of Earth's history as just one year, then January 1 represents the beginning of Earth more than four billions years ago, and midnight of December 31 represents today.

The first evidence of Earth life dates back to 3,850 million years ago (abbreviated as 3,850 mya) when our planet was 700 million years old. On our one-year calendar, this would be February 26. Single-celled bacteria were the first living forms that we know about.

For approximately two billion years, these simple microscopic organisms were the only Earthlings. During that time, they made magnificent inventions. They could move from one place to another, use the Sun's energy to make food, and multiply in numbers by copying themselves.

February 26
Single-cell
bacteria

It took life much longer to develop multicellular organisms than it did for life to get started on Earth. While it took life only about 700 million years to develop single-celled organisms, it required another 2,700 million years for the first multicellular organisms to appear. These creatures were algae that lived, like everything else, in the ocean. On our one-year calendar, they appeared on September 18.

Still just single-cell organisms ...

JANUARY

FEBRUARY

MARCH

APRIL

MAY

JUNE

In multicellular organisms, different cells specialize to do different things, such as move, digest food, and see shapes or colors. The first multicellular animals were worm-like creatures with soft bodies that appeared on October 22. The first hard-shelled animals appeared on November 18, with almost 90% of Earth history completed.

Multicellular life moved out of the ocean when plants began colonizing the land on November 27. They were followed the next "day" by arthropods (spiders and centipedes) that left the ocean to live on land. Remember that each day on our calendar represents about 12 million years of Earth history.

Many interesting things happened in the last month of Earth history (covering the most recent 385 million years). On December 1, amphibians left the ocean to become the first four-legged land animals. Reptiles evolved on December 3, and the first mammals appeared on December 13.

Birds evolved on December 19 and the first flowering plants appeared on December 21. Primates (a group that includes monkeys, apes, and humans) evolved on December 27. The first hominids (human-like primates) appeared in the afternoon of December 31. Modern humans showed up at 11:48 PM on December 31, just in time for Dr. Art's Earth History New Year's Eve Party.

Still just single-cell organisms ...

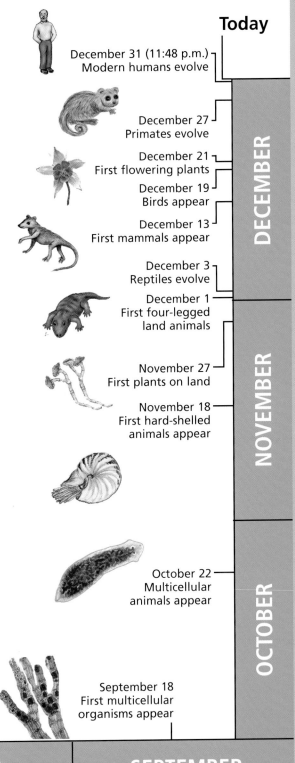

Today

December 31 (11:48 p.m.)
Modern humans evolve

December 27
Primates evolve

December 21
First flowering plants

December 19
Birds appear

December 13
First mammals appear

December 3
Reptiles evolve

December 1
First four-legged
land animals

November 27
First plants on land

November 18
First hard-shelled
animals appear

October 22
Multicellular
animals appear

September 18
First multicellular
organisms appear

DECEMBER

NOVEMBER

OCTOBER

JULY   AUGUST   SEPTEMBER

Radioactive Dating

How do we know the ages of fossils, rocks, and planet Earth itself? The time periods in our Earth History Calendar were determined using a method called radioactive dating. This method takes advantage of the fact that Earth materials have natural clocks built into them.

To understand these natural clocks, we have to go back in time, but not thousands or millions of years. We simply need to remember what we learned in earlier chapters about elements and atoms.

In brief, our planet consists of 92 naturally occurring elements. Each of these elements is made of atoms that have protons, neutrons, and electrons. I convinced a representative of each of these subatomic particles to describe what it does.

How the Subatomic Particles Might Describe Their Roles

Particle	What I Do
Proton:	I determine the identity of the atom. For example, carbon has six of me in the nucleus, while oxygen has eight.
Electron:	I hold matter together. Using the electromagnetic force, I connect atoms with each other in molecules. I also help connect molecules with each other in liquids and solids.
Neutron:	I make the nucleus heavier without changing its charge. Stable atoms ususally have at least as many of me as they have protons.

We will focus on two elements, potassium and argon. Potassium is a soft, silvery metal that has 19 protons. Argon is a gas that has 18 protons. It is a stable gas, similar to helium. In this case, having one proton more or less makes the difference between a metal and a gas.

To understand radioactive dating, we have to investigate neutrons in more detail. Unlike protons and electrons, neutrons are uncharged. They are similar to protons in size and in being located in the nucleus.

Adding or taking away neutrons does not change the kind of element. For example, the element potassium actually exists in three different forms. Each of these different forms has 19 protons and 19 electrons. They differ only in the number of neutrons. Most potassium atoms have 20 neutrons, a few have 22 neutrons, and a very small percent have 21 neutrons. Each of these forms of potassium has identical chemical behavior, making the same kinds of molecules when they combine with other atoms.

Scientists use the word isotopes to describe these different forms of the same element. Isotopes of an element differ from each other only in the number of neutrons in the atom. Their chemistry is the same, but they show some slight differences in physical behavior because their weights are slightly different.

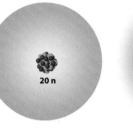

Potassium 39
Main form
Not radioactive

Potassium 40
Radioactive

Potassium 41
Not radioactive

However, isotopes can be very different from each other in one important way. This big difference in isotopes occurs if a nucleus is not totally stable. Many combinations of protons and neutrons fall apart. These unstable isotopes break down over time, and give off radiation. We call that process radioactive decay.

In the case of potassium, the isotope with 21 neutrons is radioactive. This isotope is called potassium 40 (19 protons plus 21 neutrons). When it decays, potassium 40 gives off radiation, and turns into another element, argon. In effect, a proton turns into a neutron. Potassium with 19 protons and 21 neutrons becomes argon with 18 protons and 22 neutrons.

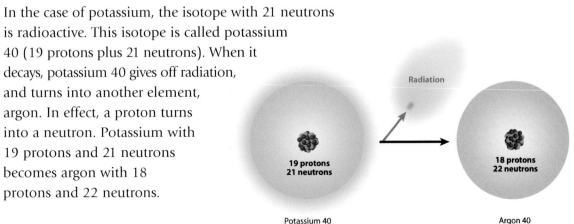

Radiation

19 protons
21 neutrons

18 protons
22 neutrons

Potassium 40

Argon 40

This isotope of argon is stable, and is the main form of the gas found on Earth. Argon is surprisingly abundant; about 1% of our atmosphere is argon gas. You are not aware of it because argon does not react with other elements. All your life, you have been inhaling and exhaling argon in each breath.

Where did all this argon come from? Back in Chapter 6, we discovered that Earth elements were made in stars through nuclear fusion. However, this process produces way less argon than the amount we find on Earth.

Radioactive dating is not about hot romance. It is a method that scientists use to figure out how old something is.

The vast majority of the argon in our atmosphere came from the radioactive decay of potassium. This metal is fairly abundant in Earth's crust. When the unstable isotope of potassium decays, argon gas can escape into the atmosphere.

By now you are probably wondering how all this fascinating information relates to the ages of rocks. Here's the clue. Radioactive decay of any particular isotope happens at a very steady rate. Knowing this steady rate of decay, scientists can determine the ages of things.

Potassium 40 has a half-life of 1.25 billion years. This means that every 1.25 billion years, half of the potassium 40 will decay and turn into argon. If we start with one gram of potassium 40, at the end of 1.25 billion years, we will have 0.5 grams remaining. If we have the patience to wait another 1.25 billion years, half of that amount will have decayed, leaving us with just 0.25 grams.

Potassium 40
1.0 grams

1.25 billion years later

Potassium 40
0.5 grams

1.25 billion years later

Potassium 40
0.25 grams

Here is an example of how radioactive dating works with potassium and argon. When rock material melts, any argon gas inside the molten rock escapes. When the rock material cools and solidifies, this new solid rock has no argon. Over time, the potassium 40 within the rock decays, and gives off argon. This argon cannot escape, and remains in the rock. Scientists can then determine the age of the rock by accurately measuring the amounts of argon and potassium 40.

The chart compares four rock samples.[1] Rock A is lava that recently erupted and cooled. It has no argon. Rock B has equal amounts of potassium 40 and argon. This means that one half-life has passed since it solidified. It is 1.25 billion years old. With rock C, one quarter of the total is potassium 40, meaning that two half-lives have passed ($1/2 \times 1/2 = 1/4$). It is 2.5 billion years old. How old do you think Rock D is?

Dating Four Different Rocks		
ROCK SAMPLE	AMOUNT OF POTASSIUM 40	AMOUNT OF ARGON
A (fresh cooled lava)	1.00 mg	0.00 mg
B (one half-life)	0.50 mg	0.50 mg
C (two half-lives)	0.25 mg	0.75 mg
D (three half-lives)	0.125 mg	0.875 mg

Earlier in this section, I wrote that Earth materials have natural clocks built into them. These clocks are the radioactive elements (such as potassium 40) and their decay products (such as argon). Scientists use a variety of radioactive elements to determine ages. In each case, the radioactive element decays, and changes into one or more different elements. Each of these decay processes has its own specific rate of decay. The measurements from these different decay processes agree with each other. Together, they provide a very precise method to determine the age of objects.

Deep Time

The Guinness World Book of Records currently lists a French woman named Jeanne-Louise Calment as the record holder for the oldest "fully authenticated age" to which any human has ever lived. She died in 1997 at the age of 122 years and 164 days. A Dominica woman named Elizabeth Israel, who died in 2003, may have lived to the age of 128.

[1] This chart is simplified to illustrate the method. Potassium actually decays in two different ways, one of which produces calcium instead of argon.

Considering that we live for less than 130 years, we really do not understand lengths of time like one million years or four billion years. Imagine if you counted upwards (1, 2, 3, 4 . . .) at the rate of one number per second, and you continued 24 hours every day (no sleeping or eating), 365 days a year. You would have to count this way non-stop for 144 years to reach four billion five hundred and fifty million, our planet's age.

Way back in Chapter 6, I used powers of ten to show that the universe includes awesomely huge sizes and extremely tiny sizes. It also features periods of time incredibly shorter and longer than we experience, from millionths of a second to billions of years.

It is easy to write or read the words "billions of years," and to think that we understand what that means. Scientists use the term Deep Time to remind themselves that billions of years are very different than hundreds or even thousands of years.

BIG IDEA

We really do not understand lengths of time like four billion years or a millionth of a second.

One reason people have difficulty understanding evolution is that we do not experience how much things can change over Deep Time. Based on our sense of time, we may doubt that something as complicated as an eye can evolve. Fortunately, we can use computer programs to model the changes that can happen over long periods of time. These programs confirm that natural selection operating over millions of years can easily produce something as complicated as vision. Life's amazing diversity evolved over the billions of years of Deep Time.

Mass Extinction

We learned in Chapter 9 that scientists use the word biodiversity to describe the variety of life on Earth. The yellow area in the illustration on the next page represents Earth's biodiversity, and how it has changed over the last 600 million years. As we would expect, the graph increases from the left to the right, indicating that more different kinds of organisms exist today than when the first multi-cellular animals appeared.

Note that biodiversity has suffered some major setbacks in its long history. During the past 500 million years, there have been at least five major times (red arrows) where the number of different kinds of organisms dramatically decreased.

We use the term mass extinctions to describe these periods when biodiversity plummeted. The most extreme mass extinction occurred about 240 million years ago. Approximately 95% of all ocean species disappeared. On our one-year calendar, this catastrophe occurred on December 11.

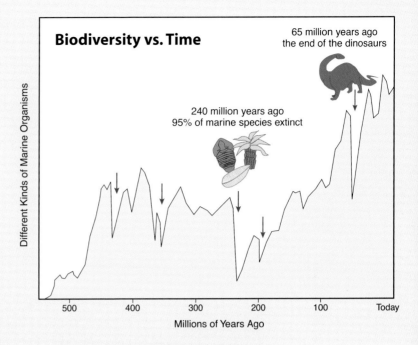

Biodiversity vs. Time

65 million years ago
the end of the dinosaurs

240 million years ago
95% of marine species extinct

Different Kinds of Marine Organisms

500   400   300   200   100   Today

Millions of Years Ago

After each mass extinction, Earth's biodiversity eventually recovers from the staggering disaster. However, the process takes time, lasting millions of years. The old organisms do not come back. Recovery involves new species evolving and replacing the old ones. Extinction is forever. Over 99% of the species that ever existed are no longer with us.

We know the most about the mass extinction that occurred 65 million years ago. We identify this mass extinction with the disappearance of the dinosaurs, but many other species disappeared. About 75% of all species that existed 65 million years ago became extinct at that time.

All of these became extinct 65 million years ago.

Try to imagine what a mass extinction means. For a species to become extinct, all members must die without leaving successful heirs. And this happened all over the planet. Hundreds of thousands of species disappeared from everywhere—all the oceans, Africa, Australia, the Americas, and Asia. Even species that survived probably had most of their population die without offspring.

We use the words tragedy and catastrophe when we speak about events where several thousand people die, or a major forest is destroyed. Our language cannot adequately describe these major extinctions that life on Earth has experienced.

Midnight December 26

Children today know about dinosaurs. It might surprise you to learn that until the 1800s, our ancestors did not know about these amazing animals. The word "dinosaur" dates back to 1842 when enough fossil evidence had been collected to show that "fearfully great lizards" had lived here long ago.

These giant reptiles excited people's curiosity. What did they look like? How did they behave? Why did they disappear?

One could mistakenly imagine that the dinosaurs had ruled the planet for so long (more than 100,000,000 years) that they had finally died of some kind of species old age. No way.

At the time of their disappearance, about 1,000 species of these reptiles still dominated life on the land. They ranged in size from almost as big as the blue whale to somewhat larger than a mouse. Dinosaurs walked on two legs, ate plants, hunted animals, lived socially, had feathers, and even flew.

On our one-year Earth calendar, 65 million years ago would be the end of day number 360. We can call it midnight of December 26, the 360th day. What caused the mass extinction that resulted in the disappearance of the dinosaurs and the loss of 75% of all the species that existed then?

Arguments have raged for decades regarding the causes of the great dying that occurred about 65 million years ago. We now know that an asteroid, 10 kilometers in diameter, crashed into Earth at that time. This space body would have been speeding at about hundred thousand kilometers per hour. The collision would have struck Earth with a force thousands of times greater than exploding all the nuclear weapons on this planet.

Forests and vegetation around the world would have burst into flames. On a longer term, this impact would have drastically altered Earth's climate for one or more years. Dust and smoke would have blocked the sun, cutting off the production of food. Acidity from the explosion would have caused rain and snow to become as strongly acidic as battery acid. The combination of global fires, lack of sunlight, loss of vegetation, major climate change, poisonous gases, and acid rain explain the mass extinction that occurred.

Iridium

The asteroid impact theory started with work done in the late 1970s by Luis Alvarez, a physicist who had won the Nobel Prize, and his son Walter Alvarez, a geologist. They were measuring levels of iridium, a rare metallic element. This element tends to hang out with iron. Most of Earth's iridium is located with melted iron, deep in Earth's core.

Ida, a stony asteroid, is 52 kilometers in length. It is the second asteroid ever encountered by a human spacecraft.

Crust
Mantle
Outer core of molten metal
Solid metal inner core

Early in its history, Earth got so hot that it completely melted. Denser elements, such as iron and iridium, settled to the interior, eventually forming Earth's core. Since most of the iridium is in its core, Earth has unusually low levels of iridium in its surface crust.

The Alvarez team was measuring iridium levels in the Earth's surface layers as part of a project to investigate the time before, during, and after the dinosaur extinction. When they measured rock material from before and after 65 million years ago, iridium levels held rock steady at around 0.3 parts per billion. However, in a thin layer dated at 65 million years ago, the level of iridium jumped 20 times higher to more than 6 parts per billion.

The Alvarez team made their discovery in central Italy. They later found exactly the same result in Denmark and New Zealand. Other scientists also found the same results at many locations around the planet. A thin layer of Earth's crust, corresponding to the time of the dinosaur extinction, has ten to a hundred times as much iridium as the materials immediately above and below the layer.

Where did this iridium come from? Asteroids often contain levels of iridium hundreds of times greater than those normally found on Earth's surface. The simplest explanation for the Alvarez discovery is that an asteroid slammed into Earth. The collision created a huge dust cloud that rose into the stratosphere, circled the planet, and eventually settled to Earth as the thin layer discovered around the globe 65 million years later.

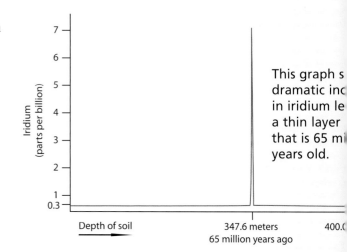

Iridium (parts per billion)

7
6
5
4
3
2
1
0.3

Depth of soil

347.6 meters
65 million years ago

400.0

This graph s
dramatic inc
in iridium le
a thin layer
that is 65 m
years old.

The Smoking Gun

Most scientists who had been investigating and theorizing about the dinosaur extinction resisted the Alvarez asteroid theory. One thing that makes science strong is that scientists will argue about different ways to interpret results. Or they will point out things that fit their theory better than a competing theory. Before they publish, most scientists will try to think of the objections that others will make, and then do experiments to answer those arguments even before others have made them.

In the case of the asteroid impact theory, scientists found more strong evidence to support it. They measured other elements that are rare in Earth's crust and more abundant in space asteroids. Again they found unusually high levels of these elements in the crust from 65 million years ago.

Some scientists hypothesized that such a large impact would produce other evidence. Earth's crust has lots of quartz, a mineral that is used in making glass. The soil layer from the dinosaur extinction time has glassy beads called tektites. These glassy beads are made when quartz grains cool after they are vaporized by high heat and pressure. The tektites from the dinosaur extinction layer match those expected from an asteroid impact. This layer also has shocked quartz, which is typically found where meteorites have crashed.

Glassy objects called tektites are created when asteroids crash into rocky planets or moons.

All this evidence and more spurred some scientists to search Earth for a crater of the appropriate size and age. Since oceans cover most of the planet, the odds were that any crater would be buried under water. Even if the asteroid had landed on a continent, the active reshaping of Earth's surface by plate tectonics and erosion might make it hard to find.

As the world tragically learned in December of 2004, large disturbances in the ocean can cause devastating tsunamis. Geologists found evidence of 65 million year old debris from immense tsunamis. The location of this debris pointed crater-seekers to the Gulf of Mexico as a possible impact area.

As in a successful crime investigation, the detectives finally found what they called "the smoking gun." A crater is buried under the sea in the Yucatan region of Mexico. Based on the amount of iridium, the Alvarez team had predicted that the asteroid impact crater would be 150 to 200 kilometers in diameter. The Yucatan crater is 180 kilometers in diameter, and it is 65.0 million years old.

Many pieces of geological evidence confirm that the Yucatan is indeed the location where the dinosaur-killing asteroid hit. Back in the 1950s, Pemex, Mexico's state oil company, had explored for petroleum in the Yucatan. They did not find oil, but they noted a buried circular structure that they thought was an ancient volcano. Later, in 1978, two years before the Alvarez team announced their iridium result, a consulting geologist examined new magnetism and gravity data, and suggested to Pemex there was a buried crater in the Yucatan. His conclusion did not get publicized, but it did eventually help a few scientists identify the dinosaur-killing impact site.

Many different lines of evidence indicate that a large asteroid slammed into coastal Mexico 65 million years ago. That event changed Earth's history. All the dinosaurs and half the mammal species disappeared. As Earth recovered, mammals became enormously successful, evolving into many diverse species that occupy a wide variety of habitats. One kind of mammal developed a science that enables that species to figure out how mammals got their big chance 65 million years ago through a global catastrophe.

One Science

I hope you noticed that all the different fields of science contribute to our understanding of the dinosaur extinction. Fossil evidence from biology told us that a major extinction had occurred. Radioactive dating using physics and chemistry gave us the age of the event. The chemistry of iridium pointed to the sky. Physics predicted the size of the crater, and calculated the enormous energy released. Geology proved an impact had occurred, and helped pinpoint the location. Space science taught us about asteroids and the science of craters.

In part, I described the dinosaur extinction because I like to emphasize how all of science works together. Everything that we learn through science applies to the world in which we live. It all fits together. I call this the Awesome One Science Idea.

For personal reasons, we may want to pick and choose the science that we accept. However, science and the world do not work that way. The science that uses geology and chemistry to put oil in our vehicles is the same science that teaches evolution.

Evolution is not something that happened long ago, and has stopped happening. The science of evolution is happening right now. When we take an antibiotic, bacteria inside us are evolving resistance to that antibiotic. That is why the doctors tell us to keep taking the antibiotic

Awesome Idea

ONE SCIENCE

All of science works together to explain reality.

even after we start to feel better. If we don't take the complete dose of antibiotics, the bacteria may evolve a high level of resistance, and make us sick again. Even worse, the same antibiotic will no longer be able to heal us.

Cancer cells in a cancer patient evolve to resist the body's defenses and the doctor's drugs. A new drug may kill 99.99% of the cancer cells. The remaining 0.01% may survive and evolve to resist even higher levels of the drug. Medical treatment for cancer must take into account how cancer cells evolve. The Awesome One Science Idea tells us that the same science cures our diseases, provides the oil for our vehicles, makes our televisions and phones work, and teaches evolution.

Religion And Evolution

Darwin realized that many people would strongly disagree with evolution by natural selection. He was a product of Western society, and that same Western society has often reacted very negatively against evolution. This science seemed to attack the idea that humans have any special status. Evolution seemed to deny the teachings of the Old Testament and the New Testament.

Some religious people oppose evolution because it clashes with readings of the Bible that insist that every word is literally true. People who follow a strict word-by-word reading of the Bible generally believe that humans were created specially by God at the same time as the other creatures. They often believe that Earth is only thousands of years old.

Other religious people of the Judeo-Christian heritage find that the language of the Bible does not conflict with evolution. They regard the Bible as a sacred text that teaches deep truths, and they regard evolution as part of God's plan.

The science of evolution does not tell us whether God exists or not. It simply indicates how life has developed on this planet. As far as science is concerned, God could have chosen to use evolution as the way for life to develop on Earth.

You may hear a lot about conflicts between science and religion, but religious people of many different faiths embrace both God and science. They experience that religion and science support each other. As one example, both religion and science teach us to regard the universe with awe, wonder, and humility.

Religion can provide guidance in areas that science does not address, such as a meaning for the universe and human life. Science cannot tell us why we are alive, or whether the universe has a purpose.

The science of systems thinking has taught me to keep an open mind about the universe. Our universe definitely has properties that are qualitatively and amazingly different from our level of reality. When we Earthlings try to understand the universe, our situation may resemble a single brain cell trying to understand the human mind.

Yet, I am amazed at how much we do know. And evolution is part of the knowledge that we have painstakingly gained.

So here we are, equipped with amazing brains and bodies. Use them well. Think about everything that you learn, including evolution, and try to fit new information in with other things that you know and believe. I hope that science stimulates your curiosity, and helps you understand yourself and our awesome world.

A human brain consists of 100 billion brain cells. Each brain cell communicates with its neighboring cells by exchanging chemicals. What could it possibly know about the human mind?

STOP & THINK

Without looking at what you wrote at the end of the previous chapter, please fill out the chart below.

EVOLUTION STATEMENT	AGREE	DISAGREE	NOT SURE
Evolution explains how plants and animals developed on Earth.			
I personally do not think that humans evolved from simpler life forms.			
Because of evolution, organisms keep becoming better and better.			
Evolution teaches that God does not exist.			
I understand how long a billion years is.			
The development of human beings was the purpose of evolution.			
The science that enables me to drive a car, get a flu shot, or use a computer is very different from the science that teaches evolution.			

Now compare your opinions with what you wrote at the end of Chapter 11. Have you changed any of your opinions? Which ones? Why?

If you have not changed any of your opinions, why did that happen?

How do you think Dr. Art would respond to this chart? The Chapter 12 section of the guidetoscience website has his responses. It could be interesting to fill out the chart the way you think Dr. Art would, and then compare what you think he would write to what he really wrote.

WHERE ARE WE GOING?

Chapter 13 –
Where Are We Going?

Superstition

Have you ever been in a tall building, such as a hotel, where the people in charge decided to skip the number 13? I have stayed in modern hotels where the floor above the 12th floor is called the 14th floor. The elevator buttons go up 10, 11, 12, 14, 15, 16 . . . Since 13 has an unlucky reputation, the owners are afraid that superstitious people will not want to sleep on the 13th floor.

This last chapter of the book describes what science predicts about the future of the universe, the solar system, and planet Earth. By coincidence, it is also the 13th chapter. Should we worry about that?

Both science and superstition involve observing the world, and describing causes to explain what happens. If you are superstitious and you just spent the night in a hotel room on the 13th floor, the next morning you will blame everything bad that happens on your unlucky room. If you spill juice on your clothes or stub your toe, you know the cause. But, really, how can the number 13 cause juice to spill?

Science is different from superstition in several important ways. First, we can often do experiments to test science ideas. Second, science results can be exactly reproduced. If you or anyone else follows the same procedures, the same results will happen. Third, science has reasonable explanations of how causes produce their effects, such an earthquake causing a tsunami. Finally, every science idea must eventually fit in with everything else we know in science.

Superstitions don't work that way. They are not predictable. Things never happen the same way. Further there are no logical connections between the cause and the effect ("spilling salt causes bad luck"), from one superstition to another, or with the rest of the world.

So, here we have Chapter 13 explaining what science can teach us about the future. If the future starts getting messy, don't blame me. Calling this chapter number 14 would not have made a difference. Knock on wood.

There Goes The Sun

The previous chapter showed how much we can learn about the past, even something that happened 65 million years ago. Science can also help us predict what will happen in the future. Let's start by considering the future of the universe.

As our universe increases in size, what is getting bigger?

Our universe has been getting bigger ever since the Big Bang. Scientists used to think that the universe would eventually reach a maximum size, and then begin getting smaller. However, the evidence now indicates that the universe will just keep getting bigger and bigger.

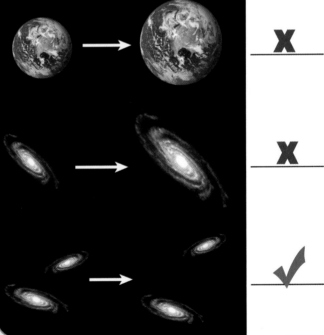

As our universe increases in size, what is getting bigger? Are the Earth, Sun or Milky Way expanding? No, the Earth, Sun, and Milky Way have stayed pretty much the same size for billions of years. It is the space between the galaxies that is expanding. This expansion of space carries the galaxies further and further apart.

As the galaxies drift further apart, they will also get darker. Stars will eventually use up their nuclear fuel and then stop shining. The universe billions of billions of years from now will be vast and dark.

We will have other serious problems long before the universe becomes dark. In just five billion years, the Sun will go through some major changes as it uses up its hydrogen fuel. I haven't mentioned ancient rock and roll groups in a while, but the Beatles song "There Goes the Sun" told about the future of the solar system.

As described in that song, in about five billion years, the Sun will expand and cook planet Earth. The oceans will boil away, and the surface will melt. In its later old age, the Sun will shrink in size. Earth and the other planets will drift away into freezing, dark, empty space.

These drastic changes to the Sun could pose huge problems for Earthlings billions of years from now. That could be their global challenge. For some reason, I am not too concerned about what will happen in five billions years. On the other hand, I am concerned about some global challenges that face us right now.

BIG IDEA

We cannot destroy life on Earth.

Save The Planet?

You probably have seen the phrase, "Save the Planet." My advice? Don't worry about saving planet Earth.

Our planet has lasted more than four billion years and survived far greater calamities than anything we can do. Life survived asteroids crashing into Earth. We cannot destroy Earth or life on our planet.

Does that mean we don't have to worry how our actions can affect the environment? I don't think so. Even though we cannot destroy life on Earth, we can cause global changes that would be very harmful to many of Earth's current inhabitants, including ourselves.

Local environmental issues.

Every day, the newspaper, TV, and radio discuss one or more environmental issues. In general, there are two different kinds of environmental issues—local and global. Local issues concern the areas close to where we live, and the things in our environment that affect us every day (water, air, food, garbage). In contrast, **global environmental issues** relate to conditions throughout the planet.

In considering the future, we will explore three issues that can change current conditions on a planetary scale. These global environmental issues are:

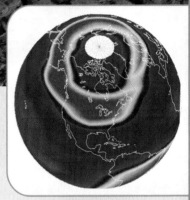

Ozone – destruction of the ozone in the upper atmosphere that protects organisms from the Sun's ultraviolet (UV) radiation

Climate – increase in greenhouse gases in the atmosphere resulting in climate changes throughout the planet

Extinction – high rates of species extinction and damage to ecosystems

Earth's Ozone Layer

This global environmental issue involves the thin, but vital, layer of **ozone** in the upper atmosphere. This ozone protects Earth's organisms from the Sun's ultraviolet radiation. Chemicals that humans have produced are destroying this ozone, and causing an increase in the amount of UV radiation that reaches the Earth's surface.

Ozone is a form of oxygen. The oxygen gas that we breathe consists of two oxygen atoms bonded together. In contrast, a molecule of ozone has three oxygen atoms connected with each other. This change in chemical structure causes these forms of oxygen to have different properties. While we breathe the two-atom form, the three-atom form is quite toxic to us.

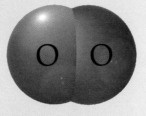

Oxygen (O₂)

Ozone (O₃)

Good Ozone and Bad Ozone

TYPE OF OZONE	WHERE IS IT?	HOW IS IT MADE?	WHAT DOES IT DO?
"Good" ozone	Upper atmosphere	Natural result of oxygen reacting with UV light.	Protects life from the Sun's UV rays.
"Bad" ozone	City smog	Results from pollutants (e.g. car exhaust) reacting with sunlight.	Causes health problems, especially with breathing.

Fortunately, most of Earth's ozone is in the upper atmosphere, 15 to 50 kilometers (about 9 to 30 miles) above our heads. Up there, it absorbs the Sun's UV radiation and protects us. Actually, some ozone occurs in the lower atmosphere that we breathe. This ozone is part of the city smog caused by pollution. It is a local environmental issue because it harms our lungs. Some people call them good ozone and bad ozone.

The difference between O₂ and O₃ shows again how a small change in a part can cause a big change in a system.

We care about the ozone in the upper atmosphere because it protects life from the Sun's UV radiation. Even small increases in UV exposure can cause increases in human diseases such as skin cancer. Increases in UV radiation can also damage many of Earth's organisms and ecosystems.

In the 1900s, industrial societies began using large amounts of new chemicals called **chlorofluorocarbons**, CFC for short. These chemicals had lots of uses, especially in refrigeration and air conditioning. Best of all, CFCs seemed safe because they do not harm people or even combine with other chemicals.

Because they are stable and do not react with other materials, CFCs started accumulating in the upper atmosphere. There, high energy UV radiation breaks up CFC molecules, releasing chlorine. Each CFC chlorine atom that is released in the upper atmosphere can destroy 100,000 ozone molecules.

Meet a chlorofluorocarbon (CFC)

● Carbon

○ Chlorine

○ Fluorine

We did not know this was happening, so scientists were very surprised when they started finding drastic decreases in atmospheric ozone, especially in the Southern Hemisphere. In response, the governments of the world agreed to replace and phase out CFCs. These agreements appear to be working. We currently expect the ozone layer to slowly recover and return to its pre-industrial level between the years 2050 and 2100.

This ozone story tells us that very unpleasant surprises can happen if we ignore Earth's cycles of matter. We manufactured large amounts of a new kind of chemical. Since CFCs could not be naturally recycled, they accumulated in the atmosphere. Eventually, these molecules harmed Earth's ozone layer. We are beginning to realize that man-made chemicals can dramatically change important features of the Earth system. Fortunately, we probably have caught this problem before it could become a global disaster.

Today's Carbon Cycle

Climate change, the second global environmental issue, also involves how matter cycles on our planet. As a result of industrial and agricultural activities, humans have increased the amounts of various gases in our atmosphere. These gases, called greenhouse gases, are changing Earth's climate by increasing the greenhouse effect.

Carbon dioxide is the most important greenhouse gas that is increasing in the atmosphere because of human activities. This atmospheric carbon dioxide is part of Earth's carbon cycle that we explored in Chapter 7 (pages 121-124). In the carbon cycle, large amounts of carbon travel rapidly between the atmosphere, oceans, and organisms.

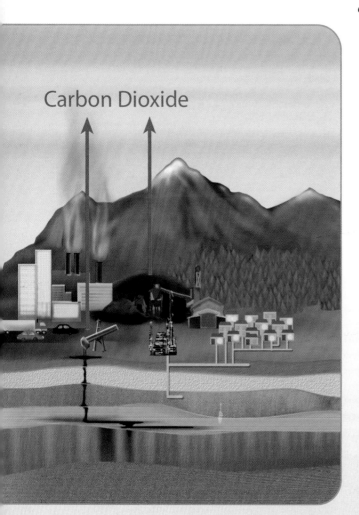

Carbon Dioxide

Fossil fuels (oil, coal, and natural gas) are an important reservoir of carbon, containing eight times as much carbon as is present in the atmosphere. In the absence of human activities, this fossil fuel carbon plays no role in today's carbon cycle because it is buried under ground. However, we humans bring this buried carbon to the surface and burn it for transportation, heating, cooking, electricity, and manufacturing.

This burning of fossil fuels currently adds approximately seven billion tons of carbon to the atmosphere. We also have been burning forests, adding another billion tons of carbon to the atmosphere. As a result, the global carbon cycle is currently not in balance.

When we burn fossil fuels, we take carbon from under the ground and put it in the atmosphere in the form of carbon dioxide.

Back in the 1950s, scientists and government officials realized that we needed to accurately measure the amount of CO_2 in the atmosphere to discover if it was changing and how much. The most famous measuring station, established on the highest mountain of Hawaii's Big Island, has recorded data since 1958.

The graph on the next page shows that the amount of CO_2 in the atmosphere has increased from 316 ppm (parts per million) in 1959 to 378 ppm in 2005. Even way back in the 1950s, we had already

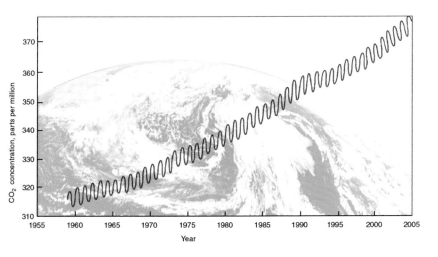

CO$_2$ concentration, parts per million

370
360
350
340
330
320
310

1955 1960 1965 1970 1975 1980 1985 1990 1995 2000 2005

Year

This graph shows that carbon dioxide is increasing in the atmosphere. Notice that the graph has squiggles going up and down each year. What do you think causes that?

Hint: the answer involves respiration and photosynthesis. The Chapter 13 section of the guidetoscience website explains these squiggles.

been destroying forests, and burning significant amounts of fossil fuels for more than a hundred years. To have a better idea of human impacts, we would like to know the CO$_2$ level before the industrial revolution.

Scientists can actually measure CO$_2$ levels in Earth's atmosphere hundreds and thousands of years ago. No, they don't physically travel back in time. They analyze air bubbles trapped in ice below Earth's surface. The deeper below the surface, the further back in time they can measure.

Using this technique, we now know that the atmospheric concentration of CO$_2$ was about 280 ppm in the year 1750, and had stayed fairly constant for the previous 10,000 years. The concentration of 378 ppm in the year 2005 provides strong evidence that human activities have already caused more than a 40% increase in atmospheric CO$_2$. The last time atmospheric carbon dioxide reached these levels was probably 20 million years ago.

Only about half of the fossil fuel CO$_2$ that we put in the atmosphere has stayed there. The ocean and forests have absorbed the rest of the extra CO$_2$. At current rates of burning fossil fuels, the carbon in the atmosphere may double in amount sometime around the year 2050. If the ocean and forests do not continue to absorb half of this extra carbon, the amount in the atmosphere could increase even faster.

This ice is part of a long cylinder that was drilled out from deep within a glacier up to the top. It is then cut into very thin slices which contain air bubbles from many thousands of years ago. The deeper within the glacier, the older the air.

231

Earth's Climate

We care about carbon dioxide in the atmosphere because increases in CO_2 and other greenhouse gases cause changes to Earth's climate. Climate is different than weather. When we talk about weather, we care if it is raining, sunny, hot, or cold in some particular place today or next week. With climate, we care about the pattern of weather over a longer period of time, and usually over a broader area. Global climate refers to the pattern of temperatures and precipitation for the planet as a whole.

Governments around the world have been meeting to discuss changes to global climate that are happening now, and that may increase in the future. This global environmental issue has more causes and more effects than loss of ozone. We probably will be dealing with global climate change for many decades to come.

The ice covering vast areas of North America during the last glaciation was about 3,000 meters thick; so the ice was six times taller than todays tallest buildings!

| Warm period – No ice cover | Today – 10% ice cover | 20,000 years ago – 30% ice cover |

Over its long history, Earth's climate has changed many times. For example over the last 2,500 million years, it has been warm 75% of the time and cold about 25% of the time. When it is warm, Earth has no or little permanent ice covering its land. That may surprise most of us who think of Earth with permanent ice at both poles. During its cold periods, Earth has lots of ice covering land throughout the year. Today about 10% of Earth's land surface is covered with ice. 20,000 years ago, ice covered about 30% of Earth's land surface.

The highest skyscraper is about 500 meters.

Many things affect Earth's global climate. The greenhouse effect, which we met in Chapter 8, plays an important role. Greenhouse gases in our atmosphere, especially water vapor and carbon dioxide, keep heat longer in the Earth system. Without this greenhouse effect, Earth would be a frozen wasteland.

While the greenhouse effect is a good thing for life on Earth, it looks like we are starting to have too much of a good thing. Global temperatures appear to have already increased approximately 0.5 degrees Celsius (about 1 degree Fahrenheit) because of the extra greenhouse gases that human actions have added to the atmosphere.

We would like to know how much the climate may change, how fast it will happen, and exactly what the effects will be. However, the Earth system is so complex that we do not know the precise answers. We do know that we are increasing greenhouse gases, that we have already changed the climate, and that global warming will probably increase this century.

The Intergovernmental Panel on Climate Change (IPCC), the international organization that analyzes this issue, predicts that global temperatures will rise an additional 1 to 5 degrees Celsius this century. That amount may not seem very much, but the coldest and hottest periods in the past several million years involved changes of just 5 to 10 degrees C. Further, we are making these changes at an extremely rapid rate. The previous warming averaged about 1 degree C per thousand years. We may be causing temperatures to change 10 to 40 times faster.

No Greenhouse Effect

Simple Forms of Life

Pre-industrial Greenhouse Effect

Healthy Web of Life

Increased Greenhouse Effect

Impacts on Web of Life

This amount of climate change can cause significant changes in people's lives. Alterations in temperature and precipitation can change agriculture around the world, affecting the food supply locally and globally. Storms and summer heat waves are predicted to increase in intensity. Increases in temperature also cause sea levels to rise, affecting coastal communities and flooding island nations. Tropical diseases such as malaria may spread to new areas.

We also care about climate change because it will affect other organisms. Changes in climate could aggravate our third global challenge, the loss of biodiversity.

Earth's Web of Life

From our earliest beginnings, humans have affected the web of life. Since everything is connected, we could say the same thing about any organism. The difference is that we now have a large population and powerful technologies that have far-reaching effects. Scientists estimate that humans currently use about one third of the photosynthesis energy captured and stored by Earth's land plants.

We are harming ecosystems locally and globally at least six different ways (see list below). In many ecosystems, we do all these things at the same time. When people move into or economically develop a new area, they build roads that fragment the habitat, cut down the forests, spill chemicals on the ground and in the rivers, bring in domestic animals, and kill the local plants and animals.

Habitat Fragmentation

1. HABITAT FRAGMENTATION
Isolating patches of natural habitat

Habitat Destruction

2. HABITAT DESTRUCTION
Physically destroying natural habitat

3. POLLUTION
Adding chemicals to natural habitat

4. EXCESSIVE HARVESTING

Logging, fishing, and hunting at faster rates than nature can replace

5. EXOTIC SPECIES

Introducing plants and animals into new ecosystems where they grow out of control

6. CLIMATE CHANGE

Increasing the amount of greenhouse gases in the atmosphere resulting in changes to Earth's climate

Now we are threatening to change the climate as well. A plant or animal species that has decreased in numbers due to loss of habitat and exposure to pollutants may not be able to survive a change in climate. If the new climate makes its current habitat unsuitable, it may not simply pack up and move to a new area whose new climate could be satisfactory. First, there may be highways, suburbs, and cities blocking the way. Second, species depend on each other. The climate in an area may be perfect, but an organism will not be able to live there if that area does not have the plants and animals that it needs for food and shelter.

Pollution

Excessive Harvesting

Species:
, a vine originally from Asia, has smothered
ntire area in the southeast United States.

Climate Change

As a result of human activities, 24% of mammal species and 12% of bird species currently face a high risk of extinction.

What is happening to the web of life today? Many biologists believe that we are already beginning to experience a mass extinction that is as severe as the mass extinctions that occurred in the past. The normal background extinction rate is about 10 to 25 species per year; the current rate is probably at least several thousands of species per year.

How can we continue our normal lives without even being aware of a mass extinction? Well, most of us live in or near cities, far from the areas where most of Earth's biodiversity exists. We live far from the areas that are currently experiencing major habitat destruction, the main cause of extinction today. Tropical rain forests that are home to about half of Earth's biodiversity are being destroyed every day.

Should we care about all these species disappearing? Most of them are insects and even smaller organisms that none of us would ever see.

Many people want to prevent extinctions because they believe that it is morally wrong to destroy ecosystems and cause other organisms to disappear forever. Many people also believe that the natural world should be protected simply because it is beautiful. Both of these arguments say that we should protect ecosystems even if they do not have any practical, economic importance.

Another kind of argument states that Earth's biodiversity has tremendous economic and practical value, and that we are already destroying irreplaceable wealth. About one quarter of the medical drugs produced in the United States contain ingredients that were first discovered in plants. Aspirin, the most commonly used medical drug, is one example. The rosy periwinkle, a plant which grows only in Madagascar, gave us a drug that cures childhood leukemia, a disease that previously killed almost all its victims.

ASPIRIN

250 TABLETS
325 MG EACH

Many medicines contain ingredients first discovered in plants.

Plants have developed an incredible variety of chemicals over millions of years. When a new disease or insect attacks a plant crop, scientists search the natural world for varieties that are resistant to that disease or insect. They can then protect important crops such as rice and wheat by breeding in the resistance from the wild varieties. When a plant species become extinct, we may have lost forever a cure for AIDS, cancer, or diseases that attack our food crops.

The natural world also provides free services that we tend to take for granted, including clean air, clean water, and food. Organisms play important roles in Earth's cycles of matter such as the carbon, nitrogen, and sulfur cycles.

How many species can disappear before today's web of live unravels? The answer is—we do not know. We don't know the details of how most ecosystems work. We don't know how ecosystems interact with each other. We don't know how different ecosystems or combinations of ecosystems support the larger global system. We don't know how many species there are today, how many are going extinct right now, and what will happen if we continue our present activities. We don't know.

BIG IDEA

We don't know how many species there are, how many are going extinct, or what will happen to the web of life.

There is one thing that we probably do know. Humans like to protect cute, exciting, powerful, and/or cuddly creatures. We want to save the whales, cheetahs, and pandas. We also like to protect ourselves. However, we and other carnivores sit at the top of ecosystem pyramids. That makes us more vulnerable to ecosystem changes.

Damage to top...base remains.   Damage to base...top collapes

The producers, who capture the Sun's energy, and the decomposers, who help recycle matter, play crucial roles in ecosystems. These very important parts of Earth's biodiversity are the plants (including plankton, microscopic organisms that support ocean ecosystems), the ugly, the invisible, and the smelly. These are creatures that we usually do not see on TV, refrigerator magnets, at the zoo, or in newspaper articles.

Many scientists and organizations now try to protect ecosystems rather than focus on an individual species. When a species is endangered, we can take that as a warning sign that we need to protect the ecosystems to which it belongs. That way, we can protect the producers, the smelly, the invisible, and the ugly, and maybe ourselves in the long run as well.

Not The End

This chapter has focused on the global environmental challenges that confront us today. Our skills in science and technology have caused global environmental issues, and then brought them to our attention. Science and technology can also play important roles in solving these challenges.

Earth systems science teaches us that three principles explain how our planet works. Matter cycles on our planet, energy flows through the Earth system, and the web of life connects organisms with each other, and with the planet's cycles of matter and flows of energy.

BIG IDEA

We may be one of the ways that our universe becomes aware of itself, and laughs.

These three Earth Systems principles help us understand environmental issues. In the case of global climate change, we are disturbing the cycles of matter by putting greenhouse gases into the atmosphere. These gases interfere with the planet's flows of energy. The resulting climate change can damage the web of life.

I believe that the more we preserve Earth's cycles of matter, flows of energy, and web of life, the more likely are our chances of preserving a hospitable planet for ourselves, our descendants, and all Earth's creatures. Through our daily actions, we affect both our local environment and the planet as a whole.

Science also gives us a cosmic point of view, expanding how we understand and experience this awesome universe. We are stardust, an intimate part of a universe that expands many powers of ten above us and submerges many powers of ten below us. We may even be one of the ways that our universe becomes aware of itself, and laughs.

Light year

Distance that light travels in one year. Much longer than a crawling second or a subway minute (p. 88-89, 102-103).

Magnetism

One of the ways that we experience the electromagnetic force at our level of reality (p. 67-75).

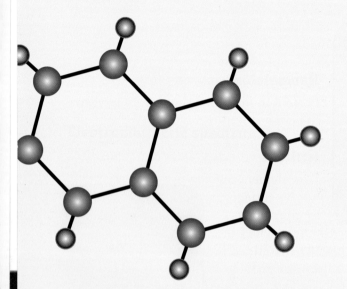

Molecule

Particle that is formed when two or more atoms combine with each other. The smallest piece of a compound is a molecule (p. 42).

Mutation

Change in the hereditary information that can cause a change in an organism (p. 197-199).

Natural Selection

Process by which populations of an organism change over time so the organism survives and reproduces more successfully (p. 194-203).

Neutron

Uncharged subatomic particle located with th protons in the center of the atom (p. 36-40, 208-209).

Nucleic acid

Class of huge molecules that store informatio in living systems (p. 173).

Nucleus

The central part of a structure, such as the atomic nucleus. Plural is nuclei (p. 39-40, 93)

Nuclear fusion

Smaller atomic nuclei combining to form larger atomic nuclei, with small amounts of mass changing into huge amounts of energy (p 92-93).

Ozone

A form of oxygen gas consisting of three atoms connected with each other. In the lower atmosphere, ozone is a pollutant. The ozone layer in the upper atmosphere protects organisms from the Sun's UV rays (p. 227-229).

Photosynthesis

Chemical reaction in which organism use solar energy to make sugar by combining carbon dioxide and water (p. 8-10, 14-16, 150-151).

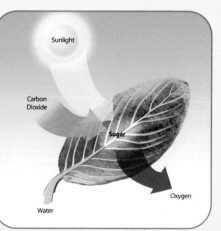

Sunlight

Carbon Dioxide

Sugar

Oxygen

Water

Physical change

A change to a material where the molecules remain the same. Ice melting is a physical change. Ice and liquid water are both H_2O (p. 56).

Plate tectonics

Theory explaining major features of Earth's surface and the causes of earthquakes and volcanoes (p. 110-113).

Producers

Organisms that serve as the base of an ecosystem by storing solar or electrochemical energy as chemical energy that other organisms can use (p. 151-153).

Property

Feature of a material, such as how it looks (e.g., color), feels (e.g., solid or liquid), or behaves (e.g., bursts into flame when it touches water) (p. 20).

Protein

Class of huge molecules that perform most tasks in living organisms (p. 167-172).

Proton

Positively charged subatomic particle located with the neutrons in the center of the atom. The number of protons makes each element different from one another (p. 36-40).

Radiation

Way that energy moves as a wave (p. 132-134). Also refers to energy released by radioactive elements (p. 209).

Radioactive

Form of an element that is unstable and gives off radiation when it breaks down (radioactive decay). Radioactive dating uses rates of radioactive decay to determine the age of objects (p.208-211).

Reservoir

Where a kind of matter is located as part of its cycle. The ocean is the largest water reservoir and rocks are the largest carbon reservoir (p. 114-115, 122).

Respiration

Process whereby organisms burn sugar for energy and release carbon dioxide (p. 150-151).

Strong nuclear force

Force holding the protons and neutrons together within the atomic nucleus (p. 78-80).

Subatomic particles

Protons, neutrons, and electrons are particles that make up the atom (p. 33-38).

Supernova

Large stars can explode and release more energy in three weeks than the Sun gives off in ten billion years (p. 97).

System

A system exists whenever parts combine or connect with each other to form a whole. The whole is QUALITATIVELY more than the sum of its parts. You, your circulatory system, water, and table salt are all examples of systems (p. 18-24).

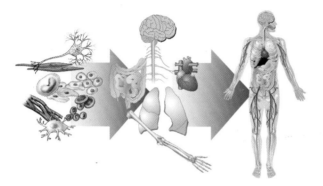

Theory

A scientific explanation of the natural world that is based on many different pieces and kinds of evidence. The germ theory of disease is an example (p. 18, 25).

Ultraviolet radiation (UV)

Form of electromagnetic radiation with a slightly shorter wavelength than visible light (p.134-135, 227-229).

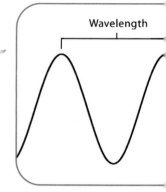

Wave

Heat and other forms of energy can travel as waves. One way that waves differ from each other is in their wavelength (p. 132-134).